inspired FREE-MOTION QUILTING

90 Antique Designs Reinterpreted for Today's Quilter

Bill Volckening *and* Amanda Leins

stashBOOKS®
an imprint of C&T Publishing

Publisher: Amy Marson
Creative Director: Gailen Runge
Acquisitions Editor: Roxane Cerda
Managing Editor: Liz Aneloski
Editor: Lynn Koolish
Technical Editor: Del Walker
Cover/Book Designer: April Mostek
Production Coordinator: Zinnia Heinzmann
Production Editor: Alice Mace Nakanishi
Illustrator: Mary E. Flynn
Photo Assistant: Mai Yong Vang
Quilt photography by Bill Volckening, unless otherwise noted

Published by Stash Books, an imprint of C&T Publishing, Inc.,
P.O. Box 1456, Lafayette, CA 94549

Library of Congress Cataloging-in-Publication Data
Names: Volckening, Bill, 1966- editor. | Leins, Amanda, 1976- editor.
Title: Inspired free-motion quilting : 90 antique designs reinterpreted for today's quilter / Bill Volckening and Amanda Leins.
Description: Lafayette, California : C&T Publishing, Inc., [2018]
Identifiers: LCCN 2017053527 | ISBN 9781617456497 (soft cover)
Subjects: LCSH: Machine quilting--Patterns.
Classification: LCC TT835 .I56 2018 | DDC 746.46/041--dc23
LC record available at https://lccn.loc.gov/2017053527

Printed in China

10 9 8 7 6 5 4 3 2 1

DEDICATION

Felix qui potuit rerum
cognoscere causas
*(Happy is the one who is able
to know the causes of things.)*
—Vergil

With many thanks to my
loving and beloved family,
Ben, Jack, and Lucy,
as I continue this quest to
know the causes of things.
—M. L.

Contents

64 Swag

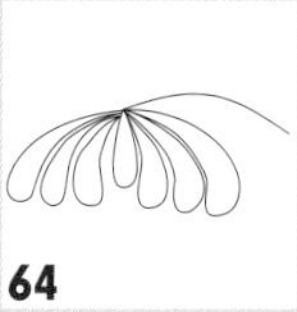
64 Large Peony

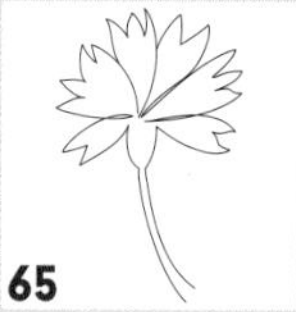
65 Aster

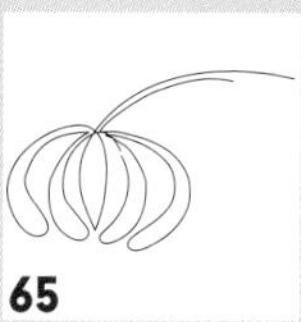
65 Small Peony

66 Album with Lyre Quilt

69 Lily Variation

70 Stacked Heart Medallion

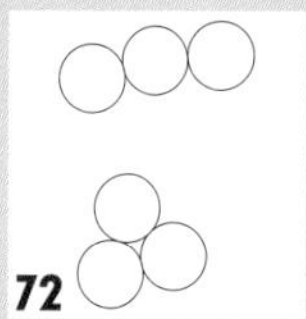
72 Pearls and Pebbles

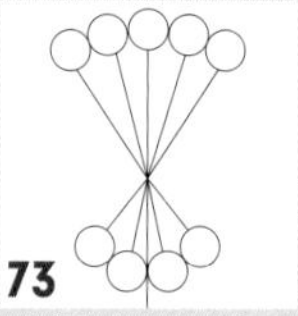
73 Haws

73 Holly Leaf Formation

73 Holly Medallion

74 Pomegranate

75 Pomegranate Wreath

75 Coxscomb Flower Head

76 Thistle Flower

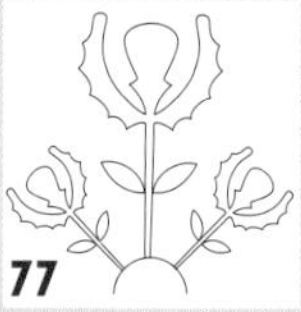
77 Thistle Basket

77 Simple Basket

77 Basket 1

78 Basket 2

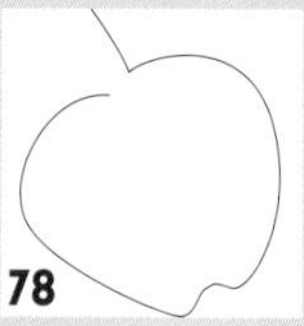
78 Apple

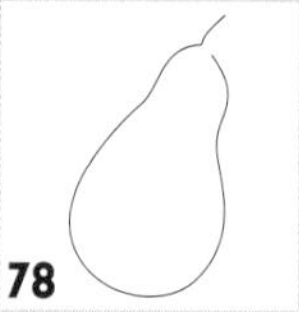
78 Pear

78 Plum

79 Apple and Pear Wreath

80 Simple Heart Medallion

81 Rose Wreath

82 Four-Block Appliqué Quilt

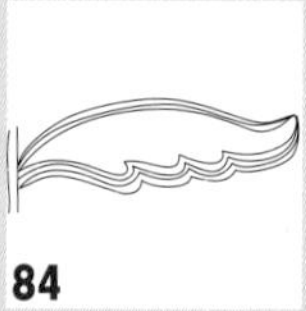
84 Appliquéd Leaf with Echoed Detail

85 Bowl with Echoed Detail

86 Heart-Shaped Feathers

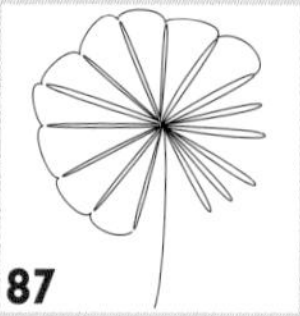
87 Posey

87 Combining the Elements

88 Appliqué Sampler with Wreaths and Birds Quilt

90 Single Diagonal Crosshatch

90 Single Crosshatch

91 Echoed Single Hatch

92 Echoed Crosshatch

93 Plaid Grid

94 Off-Center Grid

Introduction

What do you get when you team an award-winning longarm quilter with a collector who has nearly 500 quilts spanning four centuries? A book full of free-motion quilting designs inspired by classic antique textiles.

Coauthors Mandy Leins and Bill Volckening live 3,000 miles apart, but they see each other virtually every day on Facebook. They chat about everything from thrift store finds to the edge finishing details of early quilts. Both of them see old quilts as a rich source of inspiration. Sometimes they send each other links to auctions and quilts for sale.

"Have you ever seen this pattern before?" asks Mandy, sending a link to a recent eBay auction. "Not sure," says Bill, "but it looks like a variant on the Chimney Sweep or Album Patch, with the darks and lights in different places." A few minutes later, Mandy produces several repeat block patterns she created with secondary designs, all from the one inspiration block. Talk about learning things from old quilts!

Mandy's education in classical archaeology gives her a broad view of antiquities when studying old quilts. Bill has plenty of old quilts to study. The inspiration quilts they chose are simply spectacular.

For this book, they focused on a select group of eighteenth- and nineteenth-century quilts. They saw potential for free-motion quilting designs in many places, but the early quilts have some of the most whimsical, original designs.

The oldest ones in the book were made in the period of 1790 to 1810 in New England. They are sturdy quilts made of home-loomed, hand-dyed wools with hand-quilted botanical motifs and feathers filled with grids, diamonds, and diagonal parallel lines. Made entirely by hand of available materials, they are earthy but very elegant.

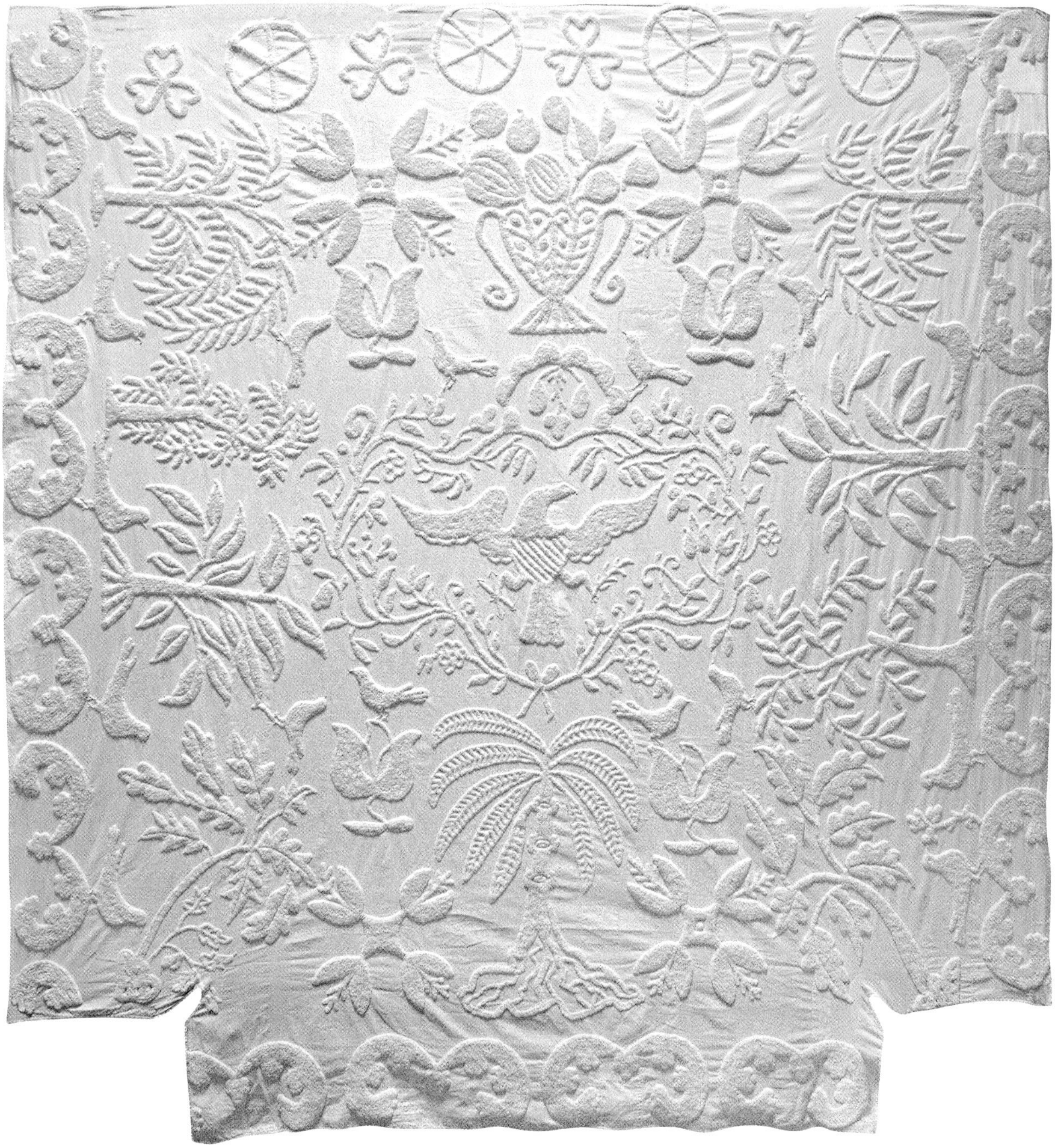

Candlewick Counterpane, cotton, unknown maker, eastern United States, c. 1825, 83″ × 86″

(For quilting designs, see Candlewick Counterpane, page 36.)

The book includes designs from embroidery, found in a stunning 1820's candlewick counterpane; stuffed work or trapunto present in a pair of quilts with large willow trees in the center; and quilting designs seen in an early geometric pieced quilt from Rhode Island. There are also designs from appliqué quilts, such as the stellar 1850's Album with Lyre Quilt from West Virginia. These quilts represent the very best of the early patchwork and quilting traditions in America.

With the exception of one very special quilt, Mandy created drawings for the free-motion patterns from photos. The one exception was an unusual nineteenth-century appliqué quilt Bill found in Portland while vintage shopping.

Four Block Appliqué Quilt, cottons, unknown maker, Eastern United States, found in Oregon, c. 1850, 73″ × 73″

(For quilting designs, see Four Block Appliqué Quilt, page 82.)

It was a rescue quilt in poor condition and was dirt-cheap, but there was something great about it. Bill bought the quilt and sent it to Mandy as a study piece for the book. He thought it would be beneficial if she experienced at least one quilt "in the cloth" while creating the drawings for this book.

Mandy thought it was very interesting. At first glance, she hadn't seen a design like that before. At second glance, the quilting riffed off the design, such as the feathery red plumes being further defined by the quilting. Together, the appliqué and quilting are one whole design. She loves that type of quilt, with the quilting and the piecing or appliqué intermingling.

The quilt helped Mandy and Bill crystallize their ideas for this book. Mandy could look at an old quilt and come up with dozens of ideas for today's quiltmakers, and Bill knew which of his quilts were likely to have a lot of ideas. Hopefully, quiltmakers would recognize and rescue the special quilts in the same way.

Bill likes to joke with Mandy about her becoming a quilt collector, and in some ways she already is. She collects ideas about quilts—color combinations, process and motifs, design sources and historic context.

Mandy says that knowing context is a good way to evaluate what you might want to add to your work. Context adds nuance, and facilitates decisions on what elements you choose to include and exclude.

Inspired Free-Motion Quilting brings quilt history and historic context to free-motion quilting by extracting designs from historic quilts. It is something old and something new. Leaving the original intact and riffing on it is the ultimate in responsible repurposing. It is how quiltmakers keep history alive.

To develop the designs, Mandy thought about how she would trace the outline from start to finish without stopping. How would it work? Does it flow or would she have to break it up in bits? She looked at the original quilting designs as if they were outlines, preferring designs that cover an adequate amount of space, so that there won't be many unquilted areas.

Mandy and Bill hope this book will be the beginning of a wonderful journey for quiltmakers who love old quilts and want to learn more about them.

Looking is learning and each person sees something different. Bill hopes quiltmakers will pick up the occasional raggedy old quilt and find good ways to be inspired by it. "If it's really unusual, don't cut it up and make it into a teddy bear. Make something new—there's no better way to pay tribute to the original."

As Mandy says, the great thing about this collection of quilts is that each one has interesting and unique features that fit together in a general historical context. The designs can either be chosen from one single quilt or a variety can be mixed and matched. After exploring the selection of continuous-line quilting designs I've presented, I hope quilters can use them as a jumping-off point to look at antique quilts more closely and do their own exploring and creating.

Using the Designs

Each quilt in the collection has interesting and unique features that fit together in a general historical context. After exploring the selection of continuous-line quilting designs, you can use them as a jumping-off point to look at antique quilts more closely and do your own exploring and creating—designs can either be chosen from one single quilt or a variety can be mixed and matched.

Look at the quilts and consider how all the elements may reveal the intentions of the maker or makers—is the quilting meant to be a part of the overall design, or is it a motif picked simply to get it done? This is particularly clear with the rescued Four-Block Appliqué Quilt (next page and page 82) and the Appliqué Sampler with Wreaths and Birds Quilt (next page and page 88), compared to the Floral Appliqué Quilt 1 (next page and page 102): the Four-Block Appliqué Quilt and the Appliqué Sampler Quilt, both appliqué quilts, feature quilting motifs that integrate with the appliqué. The Four-Block Appliqué Quilt shows an appliquéd basket with large half-leaf designs. On closer look, the large appliquéd leaves are finished off with a quilted portion above, creating a whole leaf. The Appliqué Sampler Quilt uses quilted leaves and flowers to fill out elements of the vine border. Through this interplay, these two quilts, made in different times and places, show that the maker(s) considered the work as one whole piece.

The Floral Appliqué Quilt 2 (next page and page 108) offers a different story. The simple diagonal grid (the orientation of which changes on the quilt) showcases the appliqué itself. The goal, it seems, is to display the intense amount of effort required to appliqué hundreds of circles to best effect.

While working on this book, Mandy noticed a change in her own quilting. "I've been so immersed in these quilts, it would be unusual if I wasn't affected," she says. Mandy has noticed particularly that her quilting work has become less dense over time and now incorporates many elements of design from the top itself—piecing, appliqué, and prints—to create a cohesive design that works to enhance the top.

This type of less-is-more quilting has a different set of issues than very dense quilting. First, because there is less quilting, variations in quilting are more easily seen. Second, a motif that doesn't quite work with the quilt top is also more obvious. Care must be taken that the starts and stops are carefully hidden, without the extra quilting to help. While these can seem like major issues, the final outcome is so elegant and so impactful, Mandy feels it is entirely worth the effort.

For more information on using the designs, see Putting It All Together (page 114).

Appliqué Sampler with Wreaths and Birds Quilt (Also see page 88.)

Floral Appliqué Quilt 1 (Also see page 102.)

Four-Block Appliqué Quilt (rescue quilt) (Also see page 82.)

Floral Appliqué Quilt 2 (Also see page 108.)

Tips and Tools

The quilting motifs in this book are inspired either by the hand quilting or the top itself and have been transformed into continuous-line designs suitable for machine quilting.

These designs can be completed using any of three techniques: free-motion quilting, line work with a walking foot, and line work with a ruler foot and ¼″ acrylic templates.

FREE-MOTION QUILTING

This type of quilting uses a darning foot with the feed dogs dropped (meaning they are disengaged) on a domestic machine. You create the stitch design freely—you move the fabric, the machine does not.

DESIGNS WITH LINES

Designs with lines can be accomplished in two ways: with a walking foot and/or with a ruler foot.

A walking foot includes a built-in feeding system to help move the thick quilt sandwich through the machine in conjunction with the feed dogs that are engaged underneath. This helps to feed the fabric evenly both on top and underneath. Many walking feet also come with a spacer tool to help create lines an even distance apart. For more advanced designs, it is usually beneficial to mark the design beforehand and simply quilt over them (see Marking Tools, page 14).

A ruler foot is in the same family as the darning foot. It has a high collar that is usually ½″ in diameter, and when the needle tip is centered it is exactly ¼″ to the outer circumference. To create designs using this foot, you can use the outer edge of the ruler foot with a thick acrylic ruler (also known as a *template*), guiding the collar of the ruler foot along the edge of the ruler to create straight lines and curved shapes.

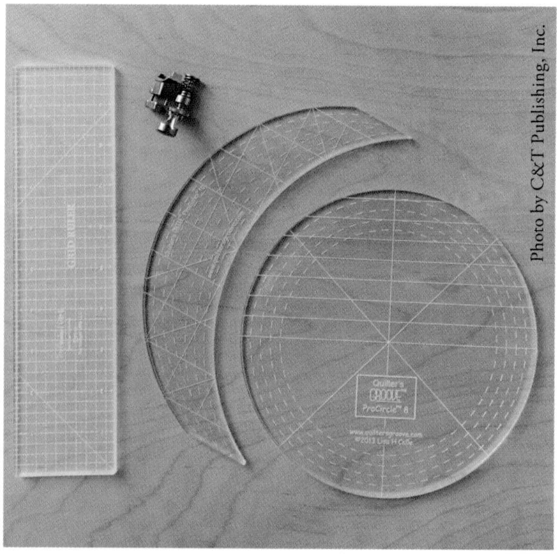

Photo by C&T Publishing, Inc.

Ruler foot and ruler

note

Ruler feet are specific to specific machines, so be absolutely certain that you are using the correct foot for your brand and model machine. Templates for this technique are also much thicker (⅜″ or ¼″ are the most common widths) than a ruler used for rotary cutting, and you can do great damage to your machine if you use rulers that are not appropriate for this technique.

TYING ON AND OFF

Many designs will have a single start and stop; for stand-alone motifs, such as a basket or wreath, do your best to tie off your threads as invisibly as possible. For other designs, such as the various grids, you will be likely be able to hide your starts and stops in the seams of your blocks. Mandy's favorite tool for tying off threads is a sashiko needle, which is a long, sturdy needle with a large eye. You can find these at many quilt shops in the hand embroidery section.

USING STENCILS

There are many grid-based designs in this book, and while Mandy shows you how to draw these designs directly, you may find it easier to purchase stencil grids. Available in a variety of sizes and shapes from square to curve, these grids provide a degree of accuracy that is sometimes hard to do freehand. With a variety of sizes on hand, you can choose the appropriate grid size for the space you are trying to fill. Center the grid on the space, mark the lines, and off you go!

Stencils come in either a stiff plastic or fabric mesh and can be purchased at many quilting shops, online, and at larger quilt shows.

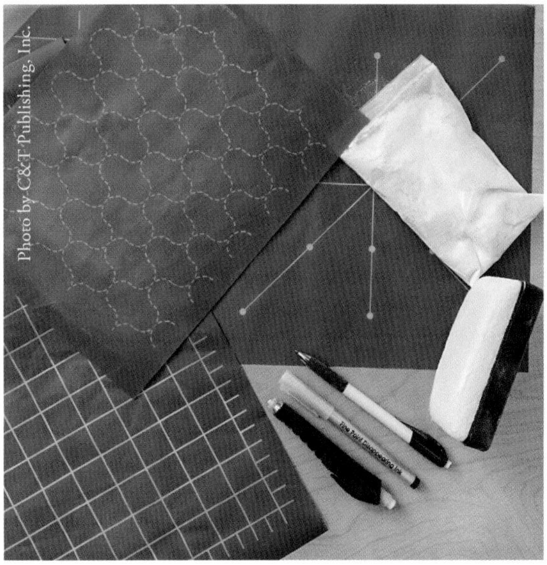

Stencils can come in different materials. These are finely woven and flexible mesh.

MARKING TOOLS

Nothing can bring a group of quilters closer to fisticuffs than a discussion of marking tools (well, maybe prewashing is a close second), but for the designs in this book, marking is often required. There are three primary marking types: chalk, ink-based markers, and fabric creasing tools. Mandy's strong recommendation is to use only those marking tools you have tested in every way possible. Nothing is sadder than markings that won't come out after all your hard quilting work is done.

Chalk

Loose chalk is the easiest tool to use with stencils. It can be wiped over the stencil using a commercially made pounce pad or you can DIY one by pouring a bit of the loose chalk into a square of flannel and tying it into a tight ball. Another option is to apply with a foam brush dipped into the loose chalk, which can help you apply the chalk more directly to the stencil lines.

The benefit of this type of marking is that it is easily removed by a puff of air or wiping with a microfiber cloth. That's also a problem, since chalk markings can disappear before you are done with your quilting. Loose chalk comes in a several colors (usually blue and white); the blue is used for lighter fabrics. Again, it is critical that you test the blue on your fabric beforehand to see if it truly can be removed.

One option to reduce the intensity of the blue chalk is to mix a small amount of blue chalk with a larger amount of white chalk, thus rendering the blue less intense and sometimes easier to remove.

Loose chalk like this can be found at most quilt shops.

Stick chalk is the chalk we used as kids for school blackboards and can be found at office and art supply stores. Be cautious, though, and avoid any chalk that says "dust-free." Dust-free chalks often include a wax or polymer to keep the dust to a minimum and that can adhere to the fibers of your quilt top, making it difficult to remove the lines. If you choose sticks of chalk, go for the absolute cheapest chalk you can find! Mandy likes to use the "kindergarten size" handheld pencil sharpeners to get a fine point on the chalk stick.

Chalk pencils come in a variety of colors, including white, blue, pink, silver, and yellow. The leads range from the very fine 0.5 mm to the thicker 3 mm. As with stick chalk, some of these have polymers and waxes in them that will ensure they stay in your fabrics. In particular, colored chalk pencils marked for tailors should *never be used without testing thoroughly*, especially if it is a colored chalk. Pink, yellow, and blue chalk pencils almost never come out after marking.

Ink Markers

The two primary types of ink-based markers for quilting are *water-soluble* and *air-soluble*. These are made by a number of different companies and all work about the same. Water-soluble markers are often a light blue ink; air-soluble are purple and disappear over time (how quickly depends on the moisture levels in the air). Both can be purchased in different tip sizes, from medium to fine.

While these are great marking tools, they do have some limitations, especially the water-soluble markers, and care should be taken to remove the marks promptly. Over time, the blue ink can leave behind a grayish or yellowish shadow if not removed promptly *or if exposed to heat and sunlight*. Heat and sunlight actually set the ink, so whatever you do, don't iron over the markings once they're in place, or leave them over a heat register or in front of a window.

After you have marked your quilt with a water-soluble marker, the clock is ticking! While you don't have to finish the quilt within a week, you should limit how long you leave the markings on your fabric. Six months is definitely too long—ask Mandy how she knows.

To remove water-soluble marker, it is not enough to drip water along the lines of the fabric. All this does is disperse the ink anywhere the water goes, like into your batting and surround fabrics. In order to adequately remove water-soluble inks, you must soak your quilt in *cold water*. This will allow the ink to dissipate thoroughly, and the cold water will not heat-set the ink.

Creasing Tools

A traditional marking tool that uses neither ink nor chalk is a Hera Marker (by Clover). This tool, available at most quilt shops, is a hard piece of plastic with a fine curved edge. The mark the Hera makes is an indentation on the fabric itself, not quite creasing the fabric. It is best for long straight lines. To use it, place your quilt top on a cutting mat, which provides a slightly cushioned surface, and lightly run the Hera along the edge of a rotary cutting ruler. It does take practice: pressing too hard can burnish the fabric and leave a shiny line; pressing too softly makes no line at all.

PATTERNS

Many of the designs in this book are based on guidelines that can be marked ahead of time, such as wedges or a grid. The several used most often are in the back of the book (Design Patterns, page 121) along with patterns for a few of the most complex designs.

THE DESIGNS

Wholecloth Quilt 1

Wholecloth Quilt 1, wools, unknown maker, New England, c. 1790, 105″ × 99″

Wool wholecloth quilts were among America's early bedcovers. Available materials supplemented imported goods in colonial America. Flax was grown and sheep were raised in New England, where some of America's earliest quilts were made of linen and wool. The sturdy bedcovers were often made of home-loomed, hand-dyed material, either all wool or linen warp and woolen weft. The fabrics were solid, there was no patchwork or embroidery, and quilts were often T-shaped to fit on a four-post or canopy bed.

Reverse view of
Wholecloth Quilt 1

This reversible wholecloth wool quilt was made around 1790 in New England. It is green on one side and yellow ochre on the reverse side. The colors are earthy, with dyes most likely coming from plants and other natural materials, and there is noticeable variation in tone from age, fading, and color loss.

Detail view of Wholecloth Quilt 1

Quilting was both functional and decorative. Well-organized motifs fit together like pieces in a puzzle. The center panel is lattice grid with rows of botanical and circular repeating motifs, surrounded by side and foot panels with undulating feathers, more circular motifs and diagonal parallel line fill. A heart in the center of the foot panel suggests the quilt was made for a special purpose.

"We never cut our threads to the past," says Mandy. "We just knot on and continue with a different color."

Heart Shamrock

1

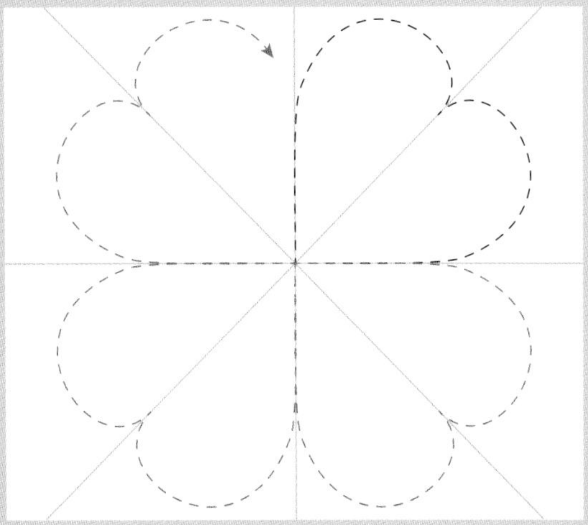

2

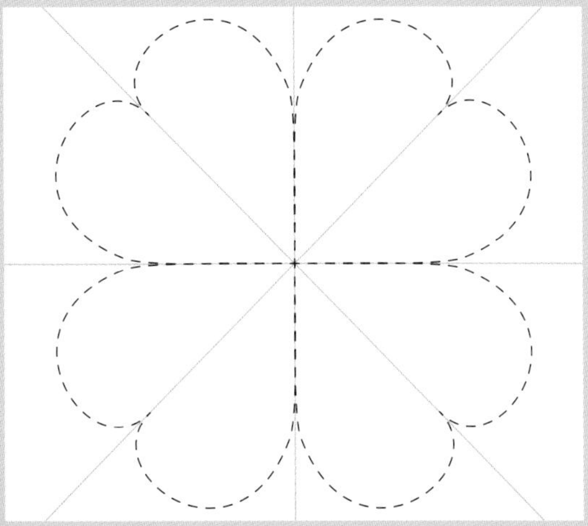

3

Embellished Orange Peel

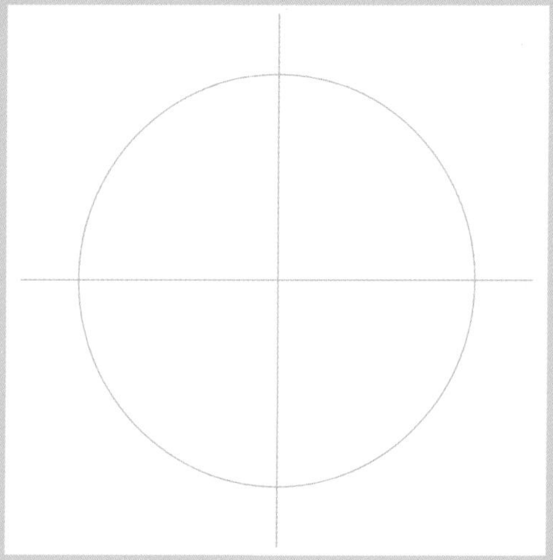

1

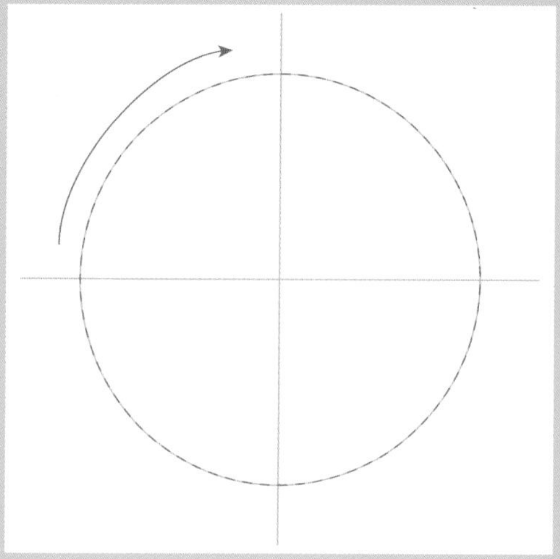

2

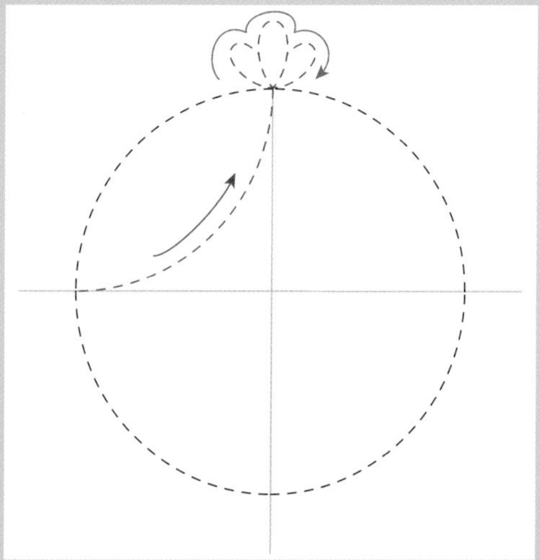

3

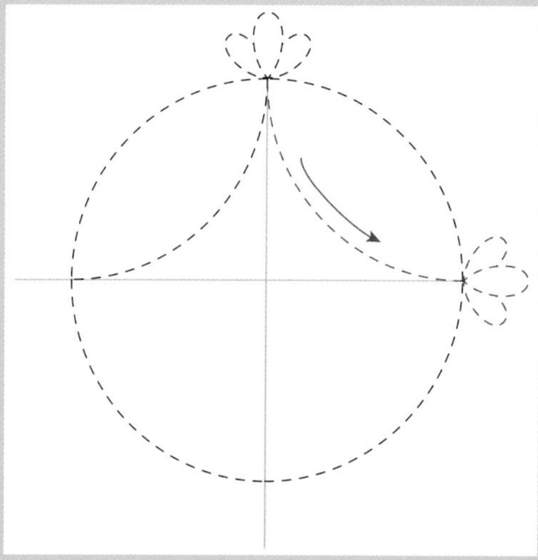

4

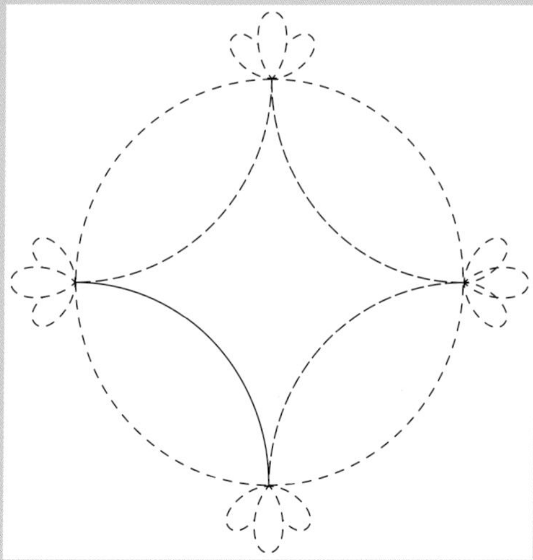

5

Embellished Orange Peel Variation

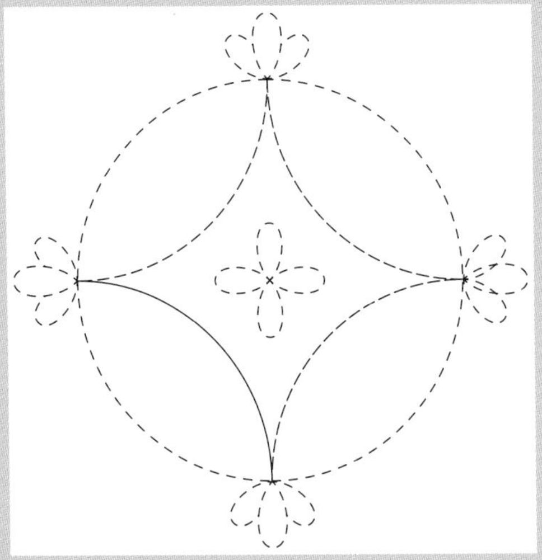

Solitary Feathers

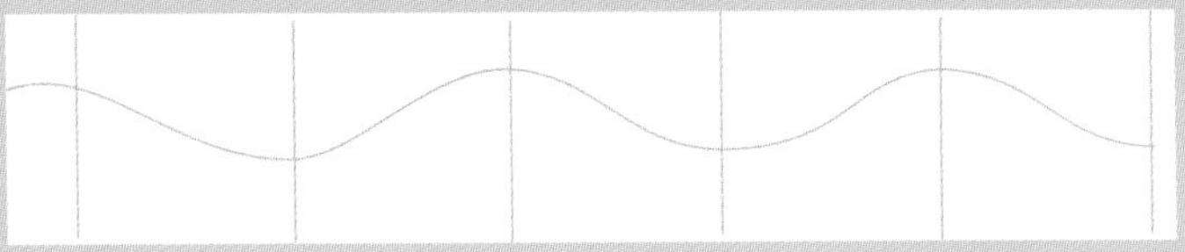

1

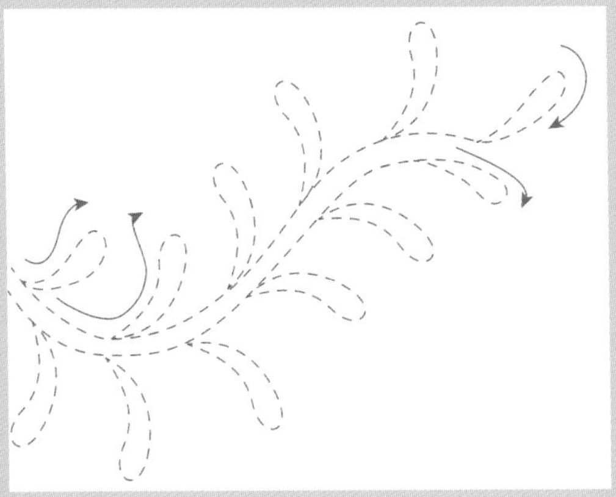

2

While the feathers in this example are more or less opposite each other, you may need to add an extra feather on outer curves to avoid unsightly gaps.

3

Complete one side, then continue to the other. Shallower curved spines are easier to fill with feathers.

Wholecloth Quilt 2

Wholecloth Quilt 2, wools and linen, unknown maker, New England, c. 1790, 96″ × 98″

Wool wholecloth quilts were popular in New England in the middle to late eighteenth century and early nineteenth century. This T-shaped, wholecloth quilt was made around 1790 in New England. It is reddish brown with a cream-colored fabric on the reverse side. A small hole in the back of the quilt reveals the underside of the top fabric, which is more of a brick red color. The quilting was done with dark reddish thread, which shows beautifully on the light-colored back.

Detail view from reverse side shows clusters of hearts.

Quilting was the only decorative element, and it was so flamboyant, nothing else was needed. Clusters of eight hearts fit together to form four-pointed stars, which filled the negative spaces in a lattice grid created by columns of spectacular, undulating feathers. Cascading down the center is a column of heart clusters with no quilting inside the hearts, making them stand out.

Simple Heart Medallion

1

For this design, divide your block into 4 quarters from corner to corner. Using the Simple Heart Medallion pattern (page 126), enlarge the design to the size you need and draw it out. Then follow the stitch pattern.

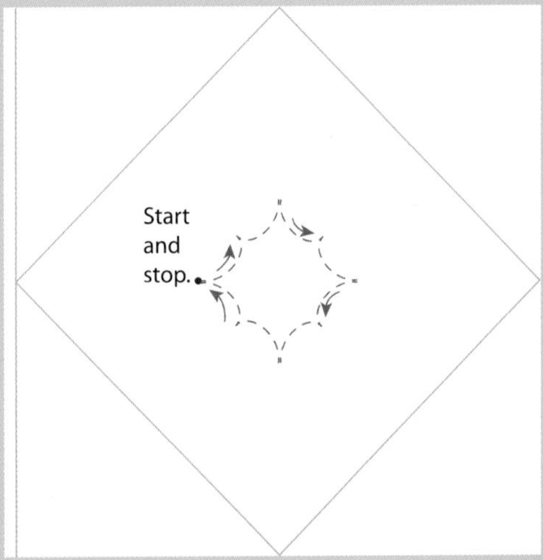

2

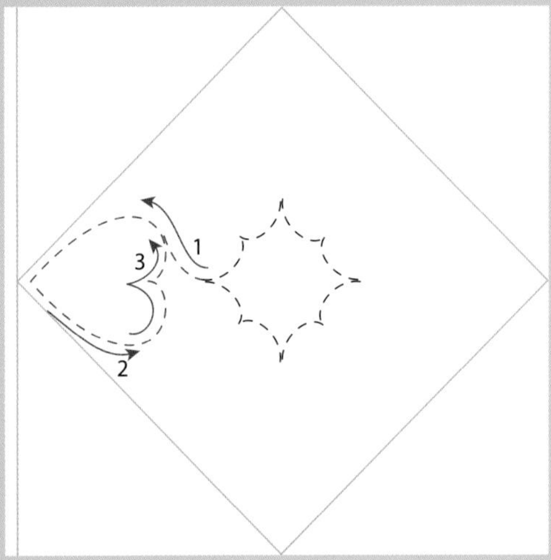

3

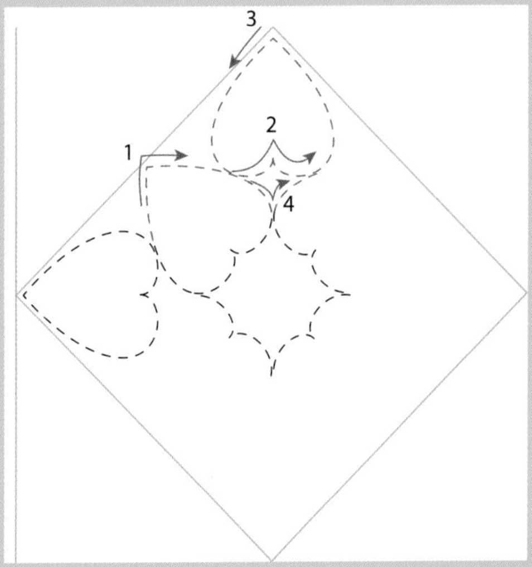

4

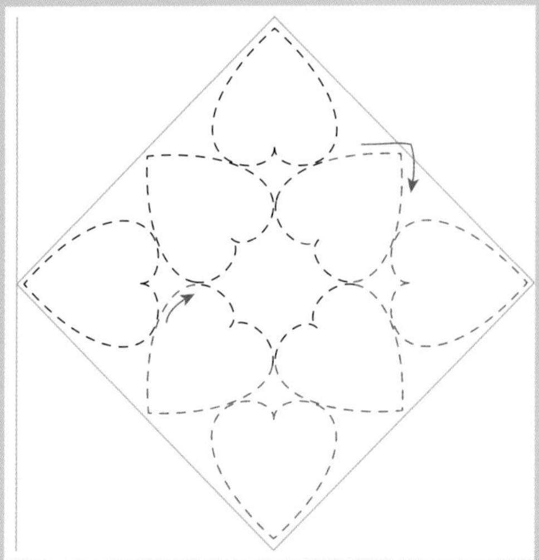

5

Feather Heart Medallion Variation 1

The interior feathers are formed as you come to the point of each heart.

A simple and beautiful heart design, this motif nevertheless requires a pattern to complete, and careful stitching. The design is begun by completing the lobes of the interior ring of hearts, then moving to the outer ring of hearts. It is a good idea to practice drawing this before you take it to your quilt top.

Wholecloth Quilt 3

Wholecloth Quilt 3, wools, unknown maker, New England, c. 1790, 69½″ × 75″

American wool wholecloth quilts of the middle to late eighteenth century include some of the earliest versions of popular quilting motifs, designs seen later in patchwork. One of those designs was Orange Peel (or Robbing Peter to Pay Paul) and included overlapping circles as the primary motif.

Like the first two examples in the book, this quilt was made around 1790 in New England. It is rectangular rather than T-shaped and smaller than the other two examples. The quilting design is simple but well planned—it includes a series of circles anchored by double rows of stitching in a lattice grid. Circles are filled with diagonal parallel lines and diamond grid alternating by row.

Heirloom Feathers

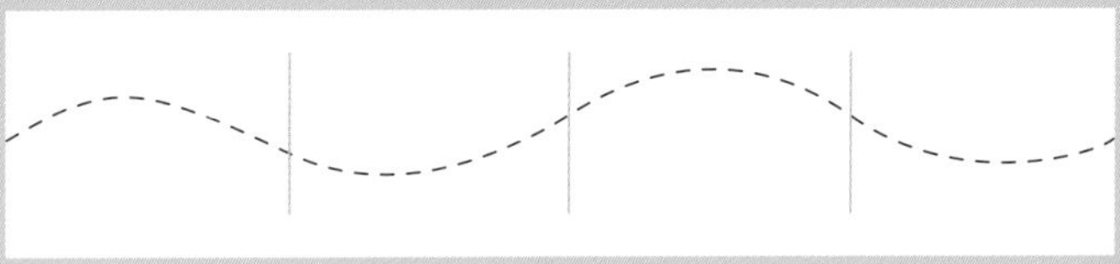

1

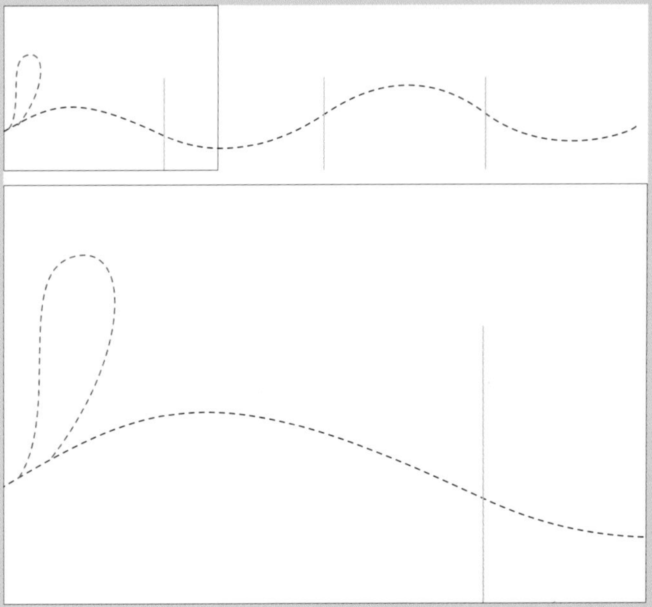

2

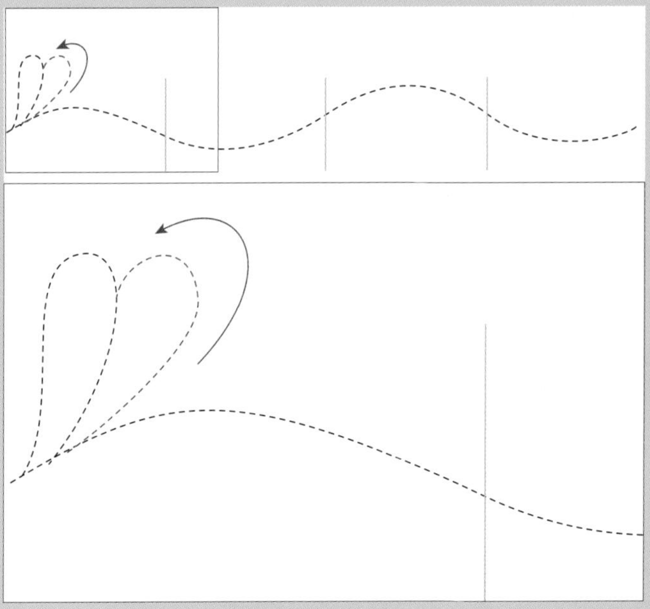

3

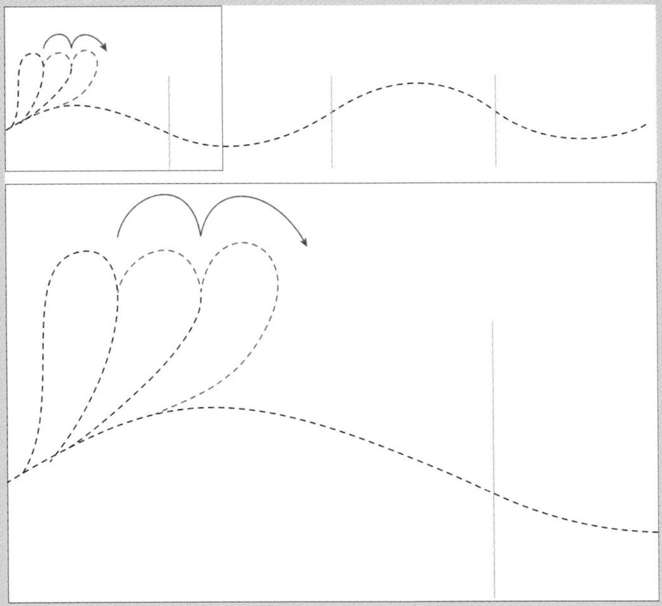

4

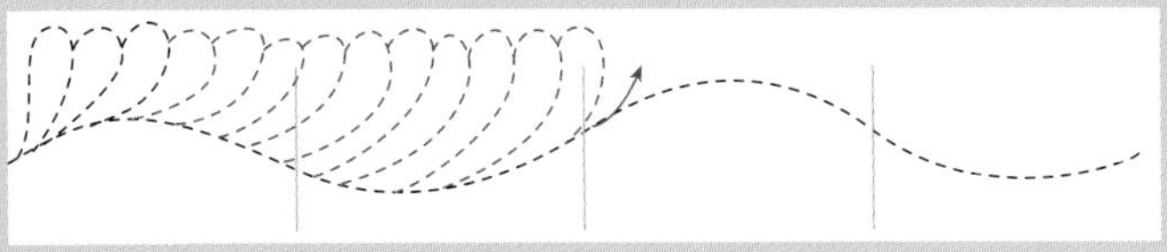

5

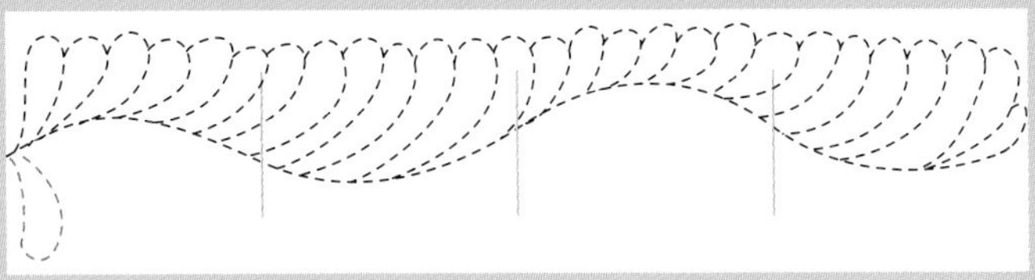

6

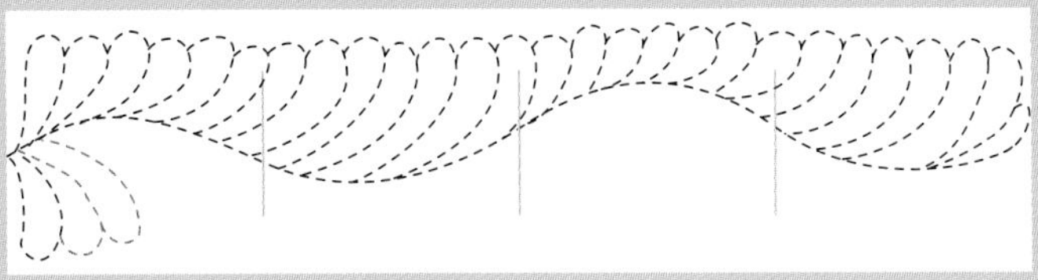

7

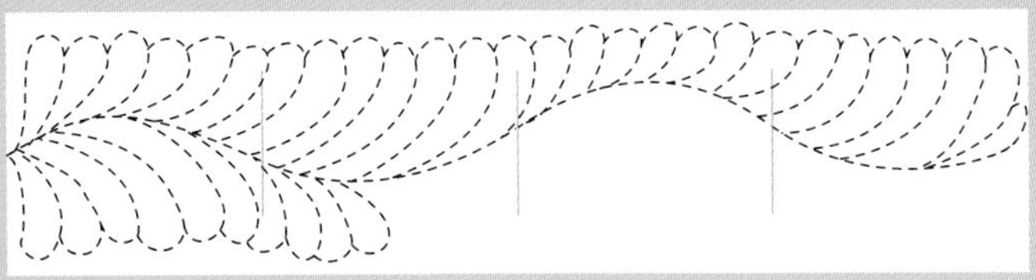

8

Geometric Pieced Quilt

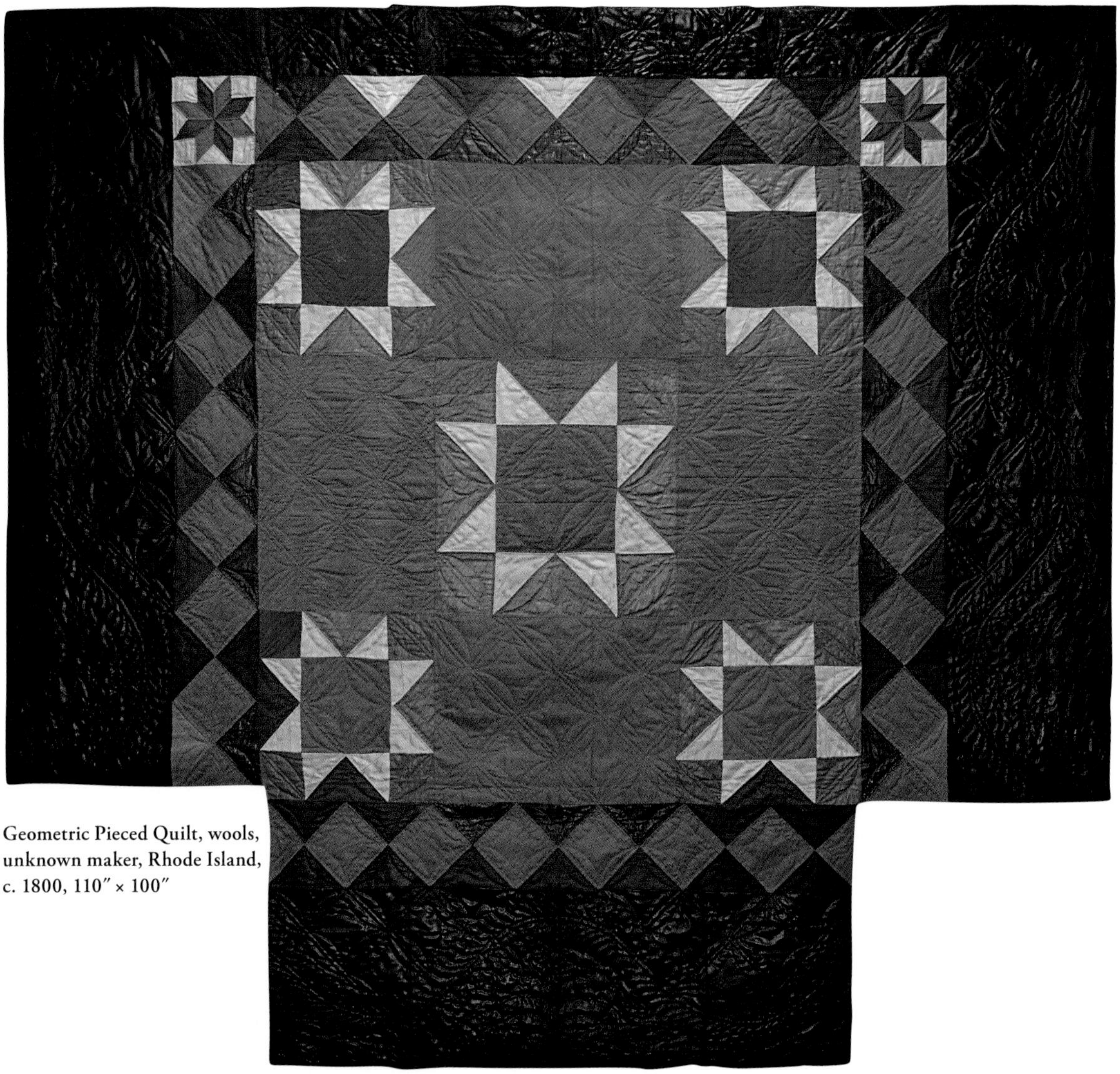

Geometric Pieced Quilt, wools, unknown maker, Rhode Island, c. 1800, 110″ × 100″

Geometric pieced quilts were first made in America around 1800 and some of the earliest examples were made of wools. Among the materials were coarse, home-loomed fabrics and other types of durable materials, such as calendered wool, also found in early wholecloth quilts.

Calendering, a finishing process involving heat and pressure, would produce fabrics with a distinct sheen. The lustrous quality helped show off decorative quilting. This rare, early geometric pieced quilt from Rhode Island includes a variety of wools in several rich colors, and blue calendered wool in the side and foot panels.

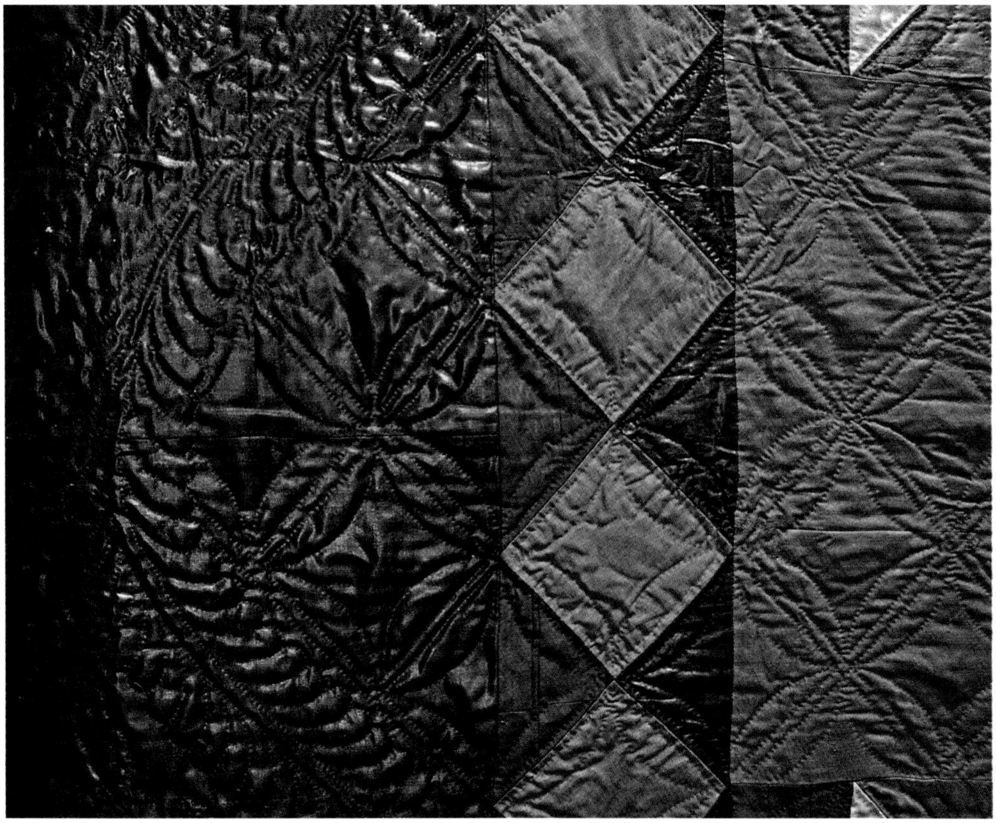

Detail view shows shiny surface of calendared wool.

The patchwork was symmetrical and organized, even in the absence of enough coordinating fabric to complete the borders and match all the blocks. The frugal use of fabric was less obvious in the presence of beautiful decorative quilting. The undulating feather vines in the calendared wool panels are especially outstanding.

The designs on this quilt are perfectly suited for hand quilting, but with some careful marking and/or ruler work, you can recreate these in a single continuous line. Pay close attention to the order of stitching!

Doubled Lines and Orange Peel

1

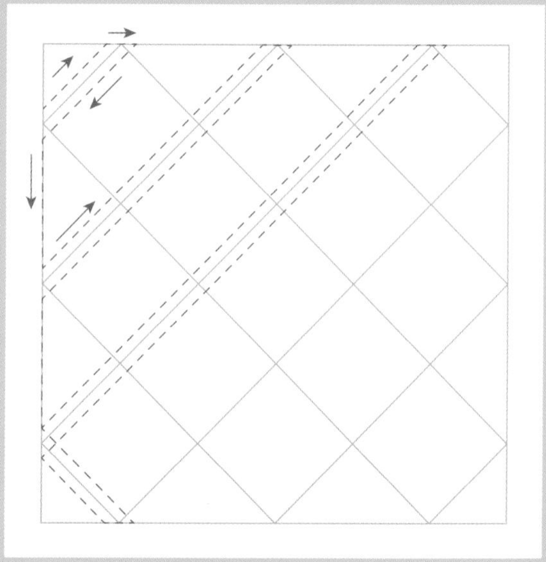

Begin by marking your guidelines, as indicated by gray lines.

2

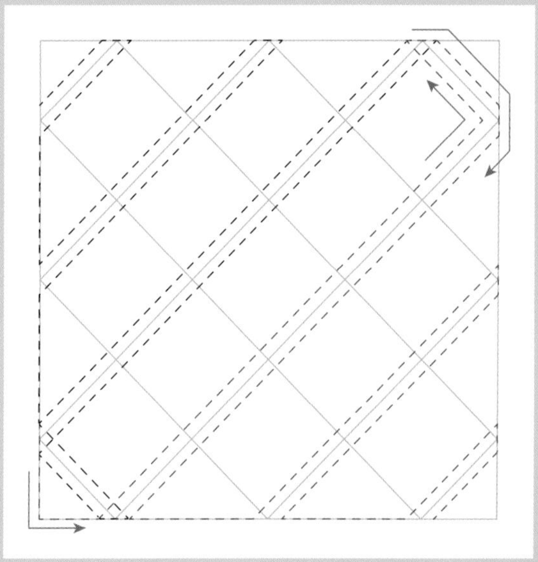

3

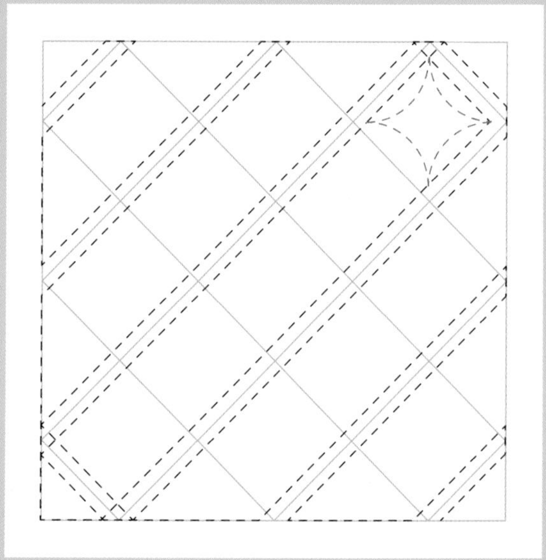

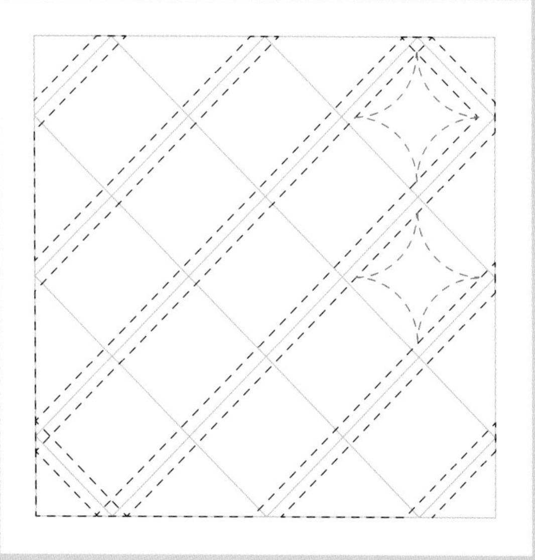

4

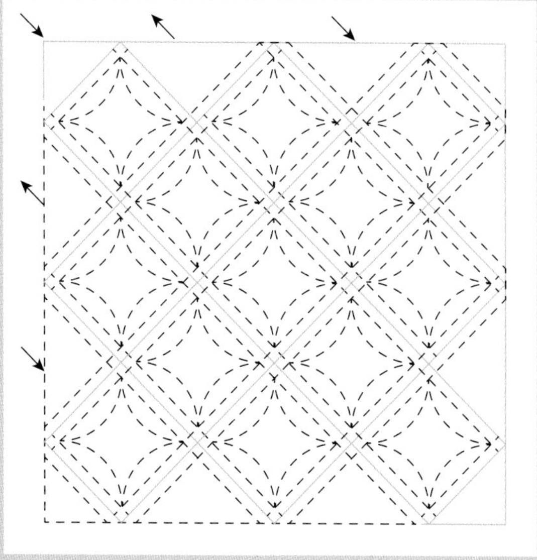

5

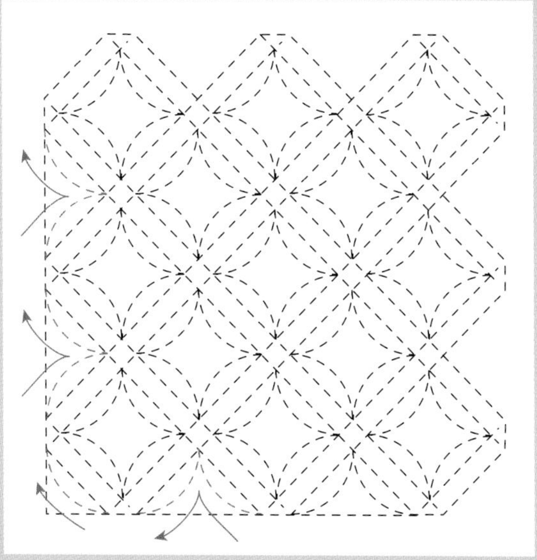

6

7

Candlewick Counterpane

Candlewick Counterpane, cottons, unknown maker,
Eastern United States, c. 1825, 83″ × 86″

Candlewicking is a type of embroidery seen in American decorative bedcoverings of the early to middle nineteenth century and in mass-produced pieces of the late nineteenth century and beyond. These bedcoverings are usually single-layer spreads rather than quilts with three layers, and they are often whitework.

This magnificent candlewick counterpane was made around 1825. It is an embroidered, single-layer spread, and it is a one-of-a-kind original. At the center is a shielded eagle carrying arrows and olive branches in its talons. Botanical elements, a palm tree, willow trees, cloverleaves, birds, and wheels surround this patriotic motif. It is rich with inspiration for free-motion quilting designs.

Basket Variation 1

1
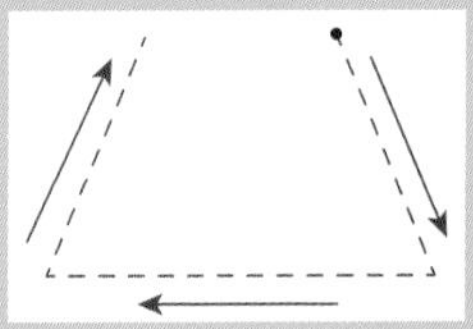

2
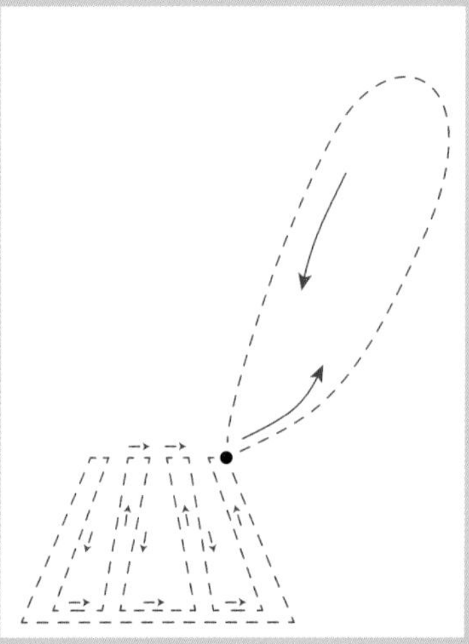

3
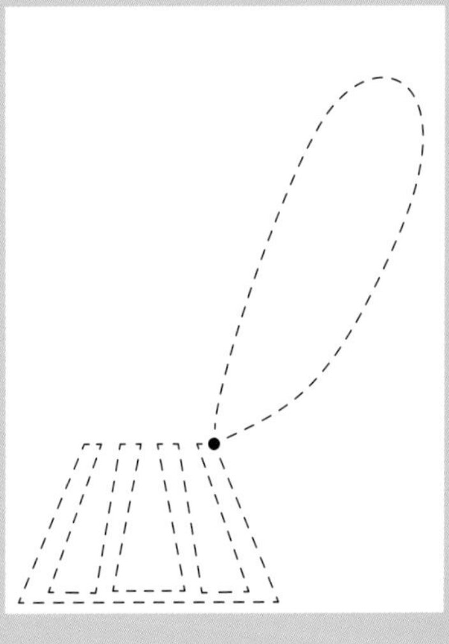

4
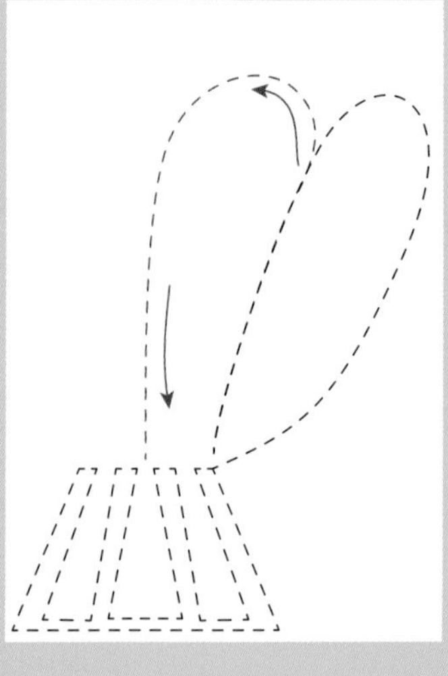

5
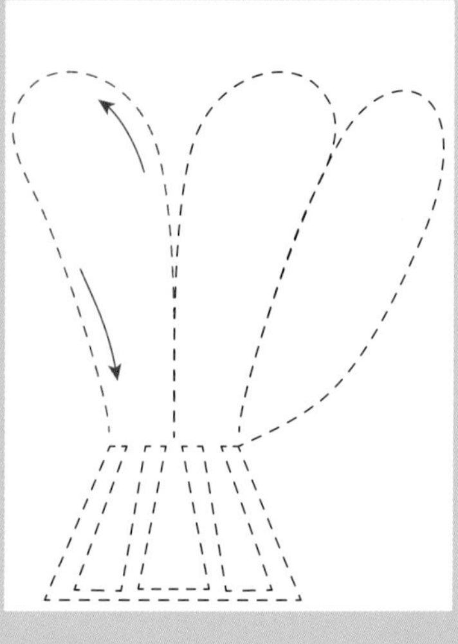

6

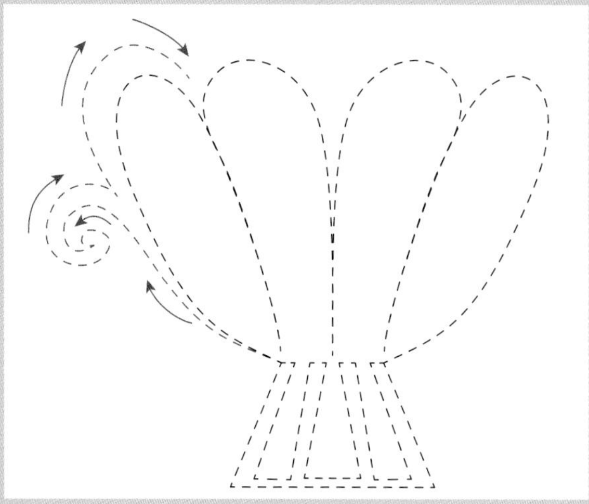

7

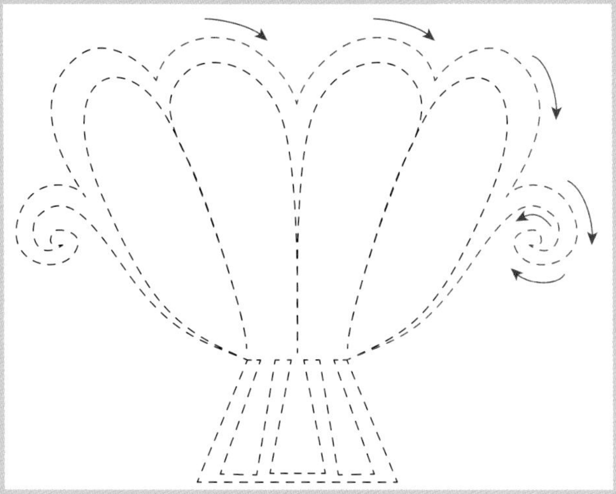

8

9

Basket Variation 2

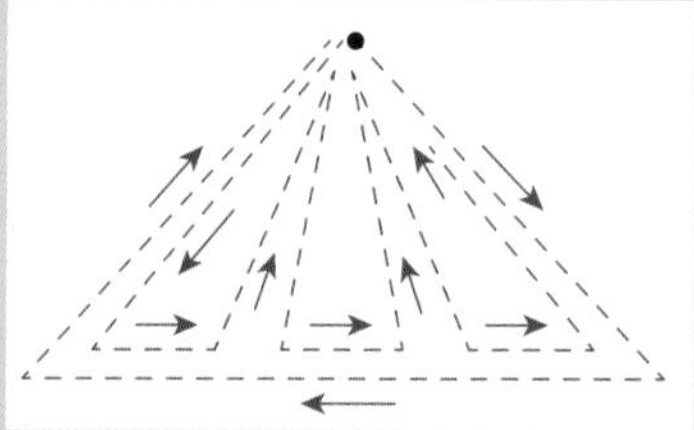

1

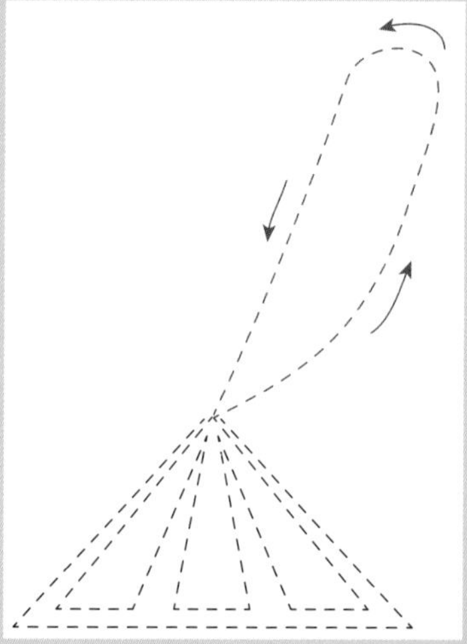

2

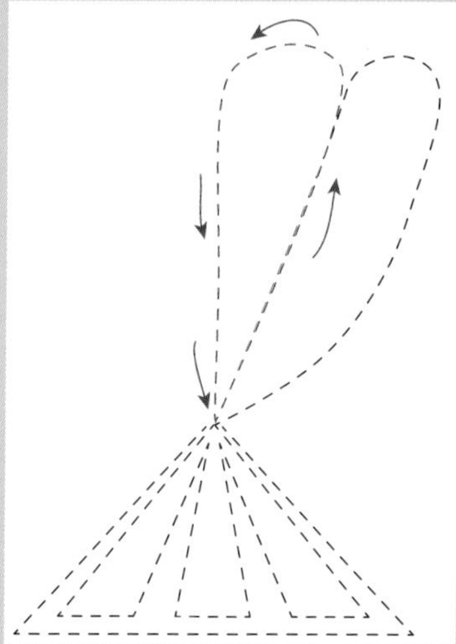

3

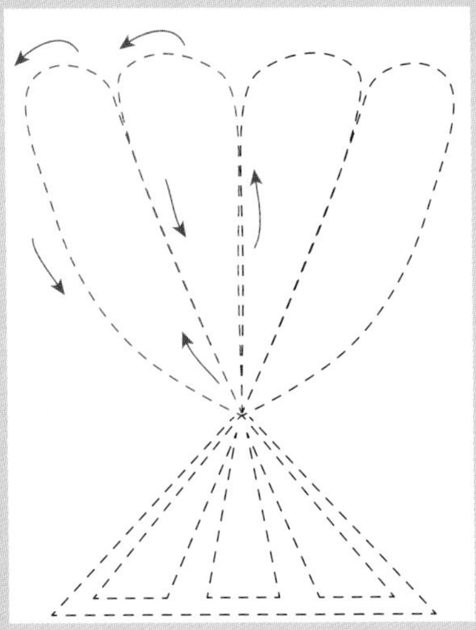

4

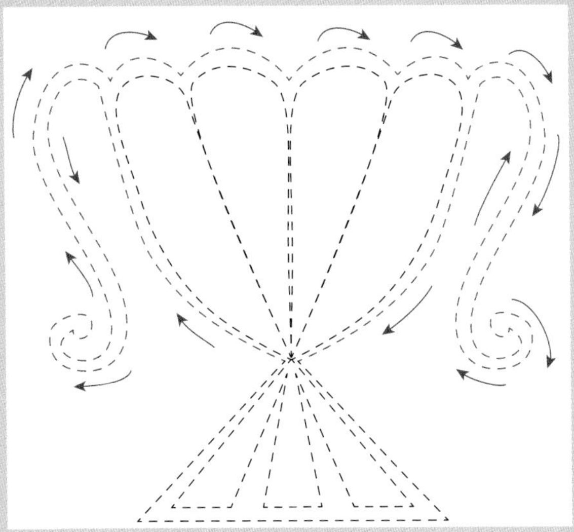

5

6

Bud Medallion

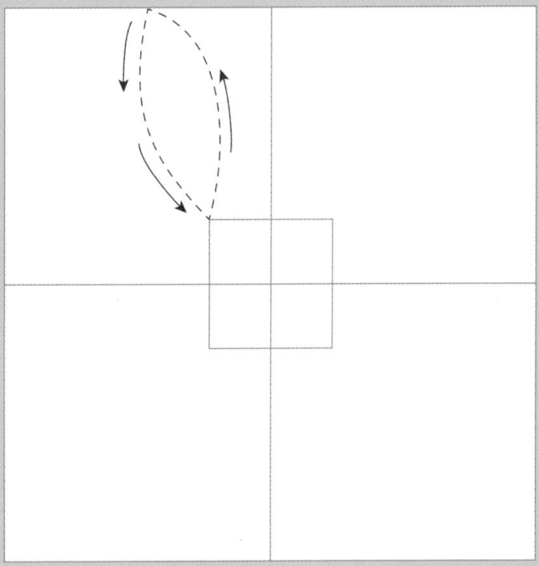

1

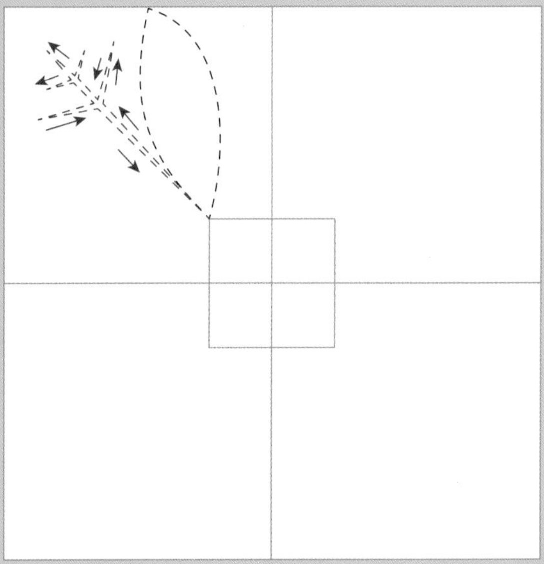

2

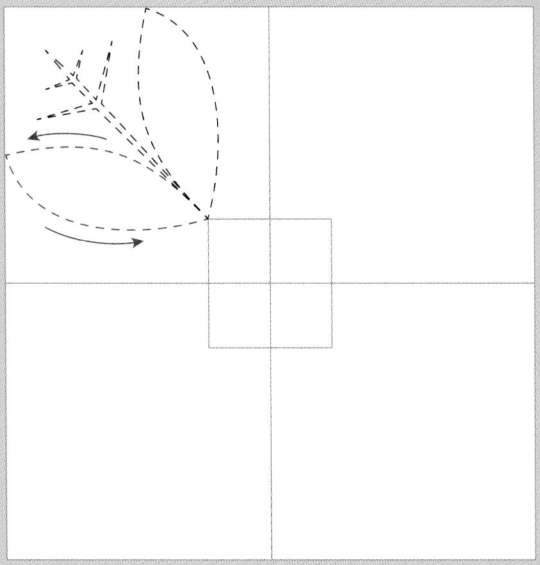
3

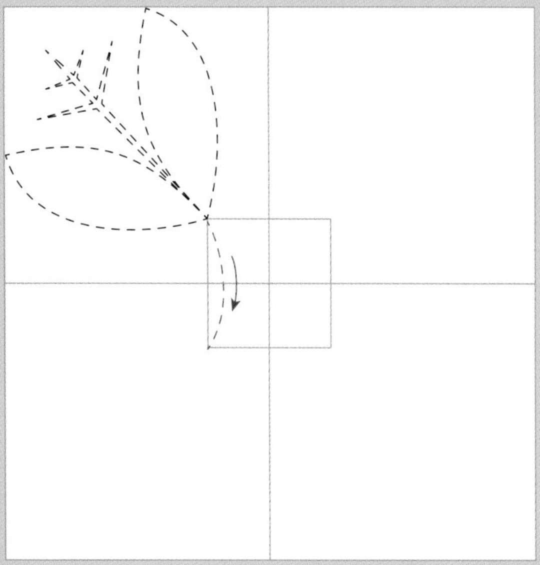
4

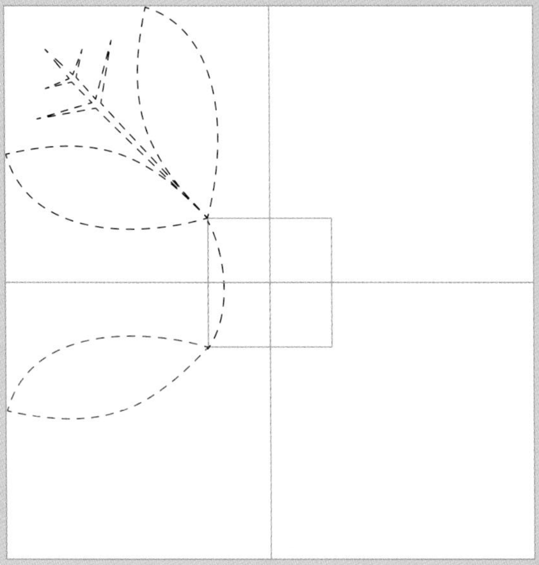
5

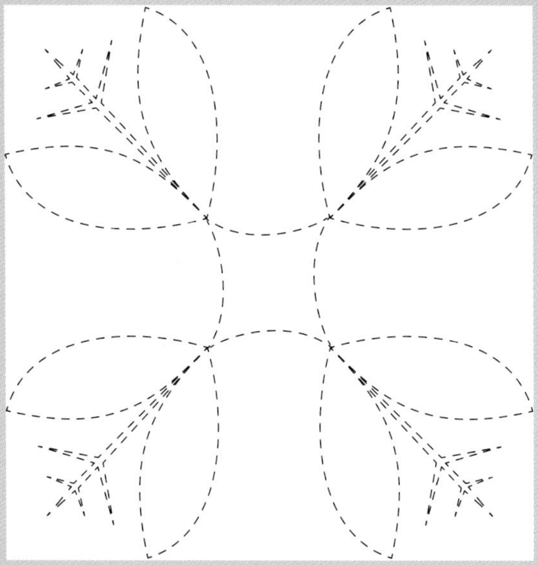
6

Tulip

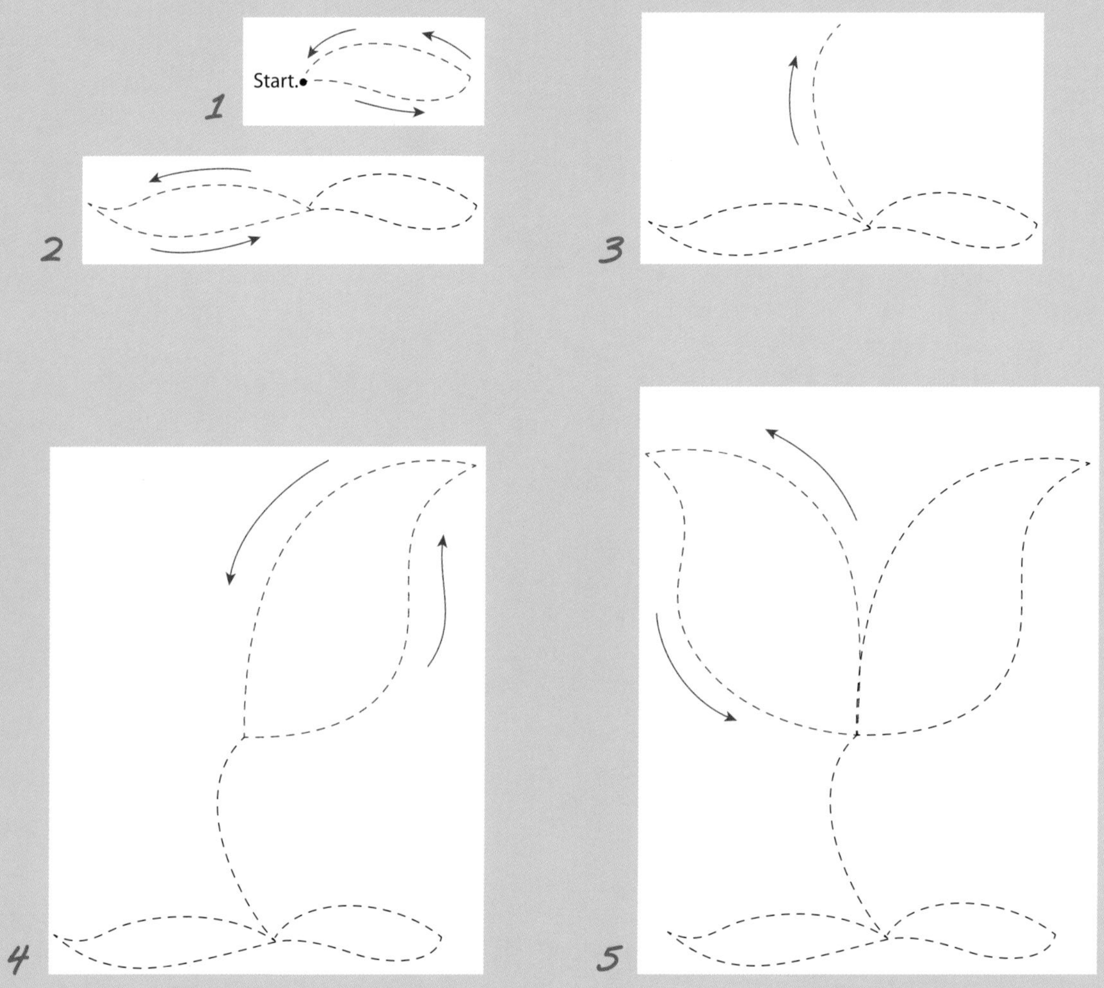

6

7

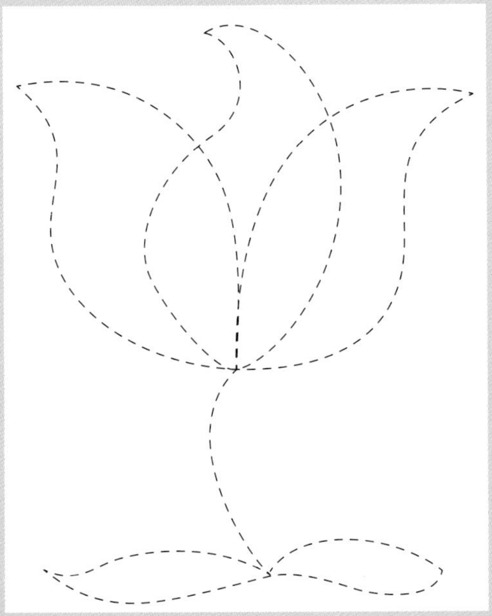

8

Feather Swag

1

2
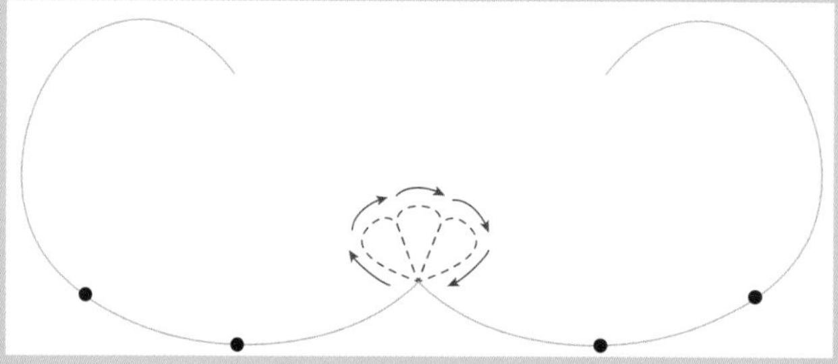

3
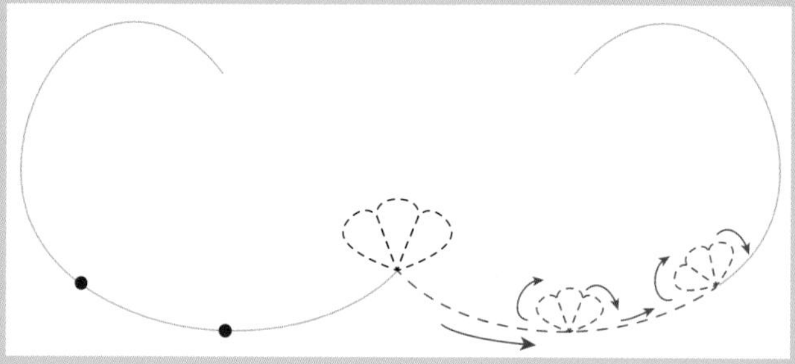

4
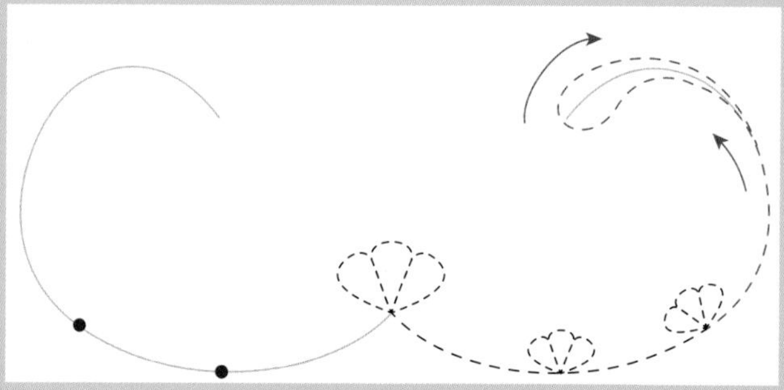

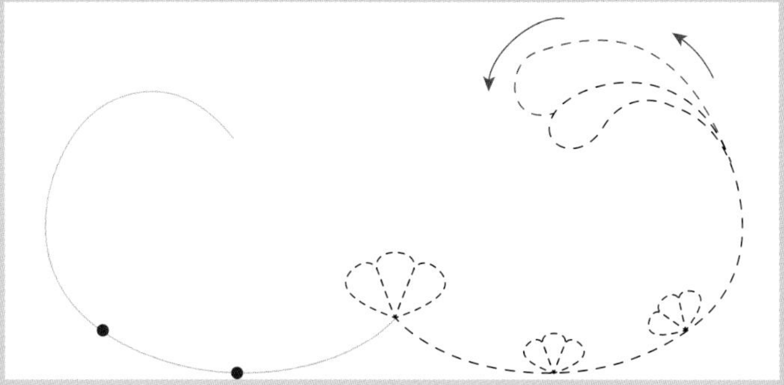

5

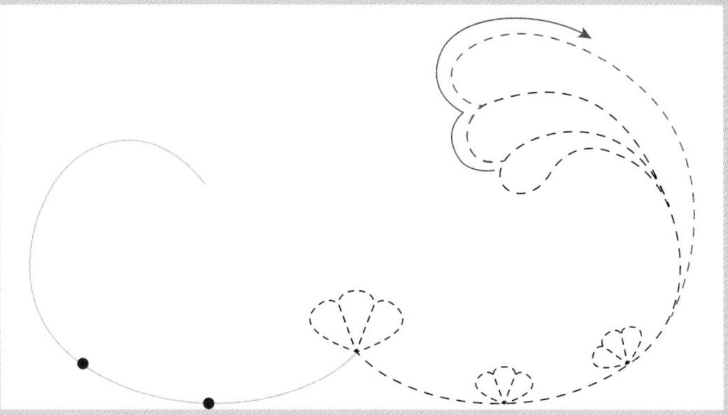

6

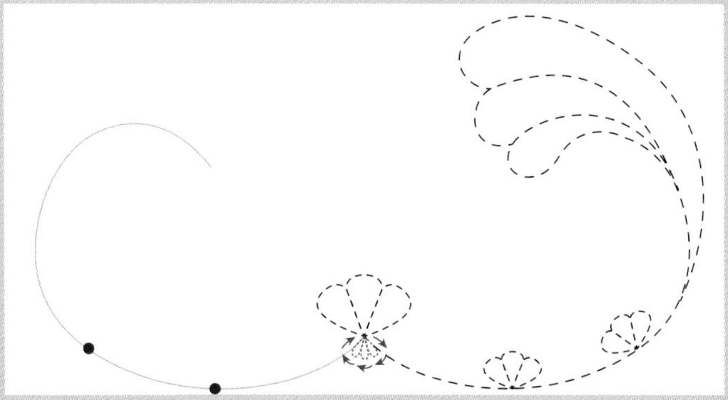

7

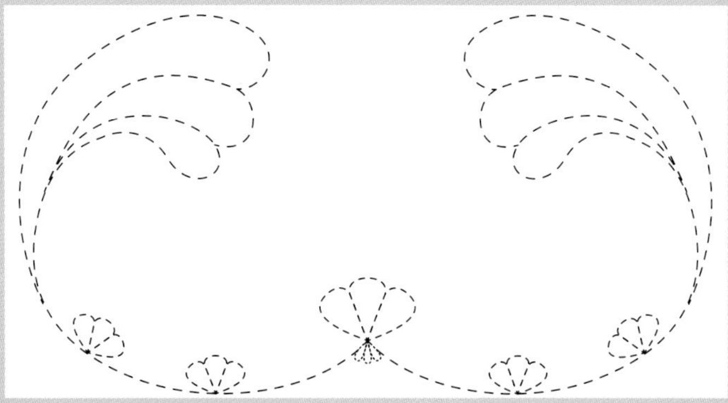

8

Shamrock

1
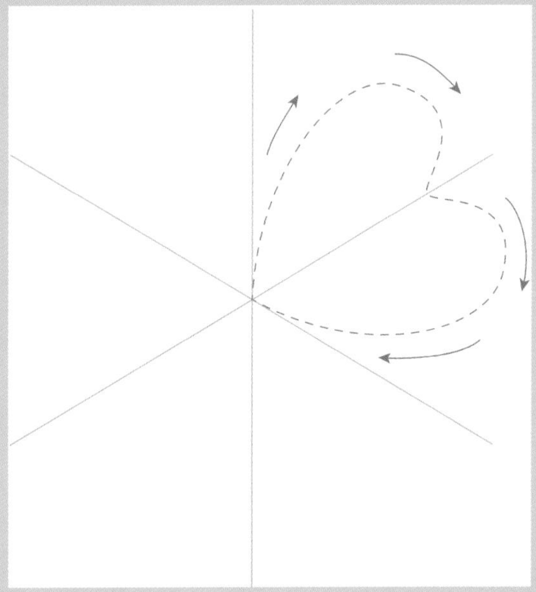

2

Tree Base for Lobster Claw

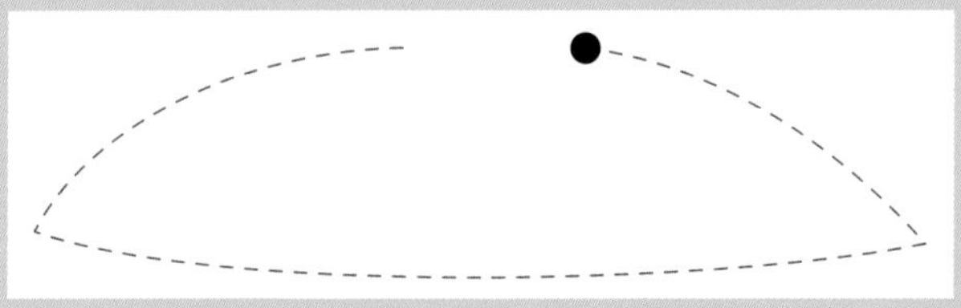

Lobster Claw Leaf Formation

1

2
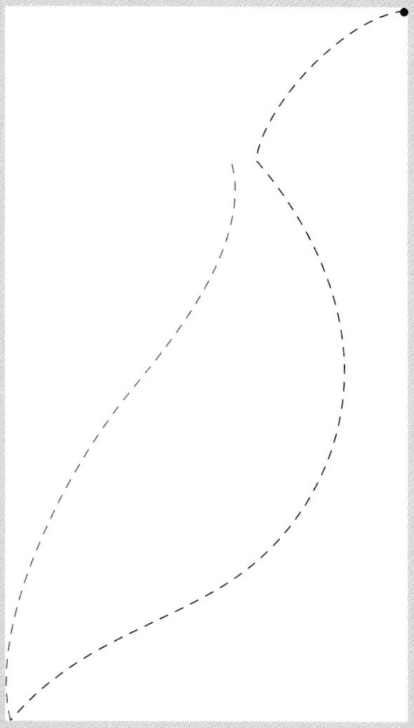

Forming the vein of the leaf instead of the top allows for an open stem.

3
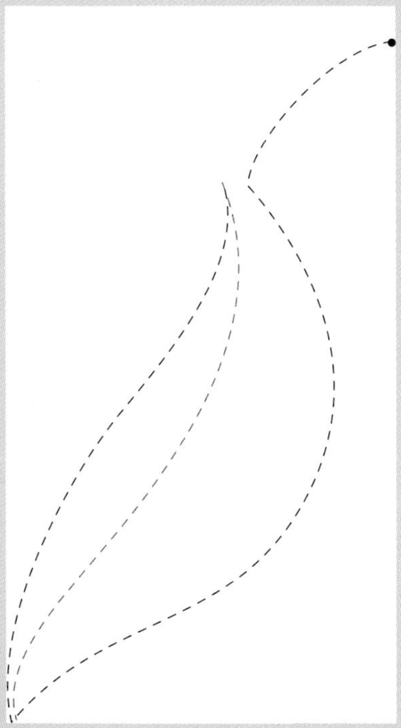

4
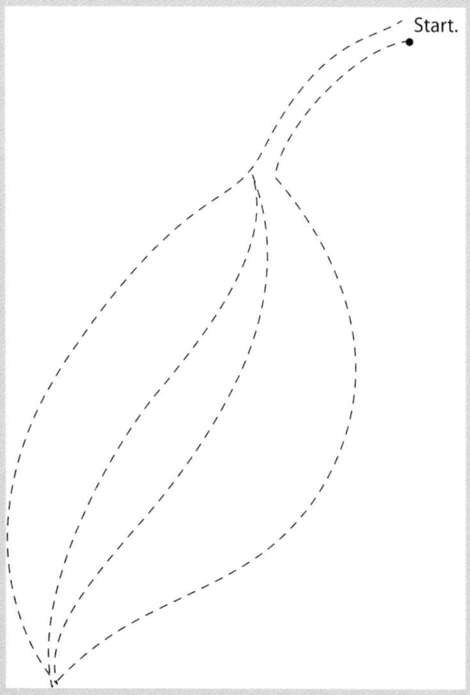

Lobster Claw Tree

1
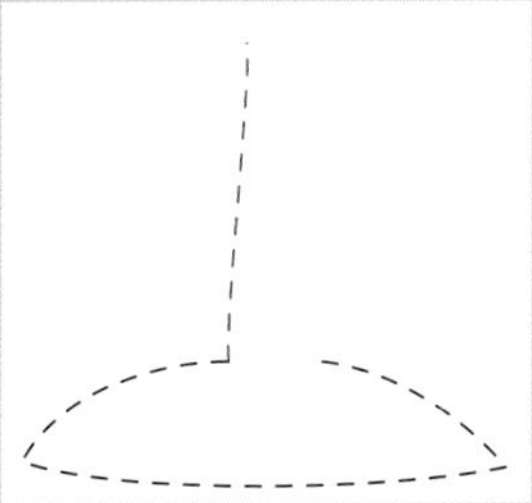

2
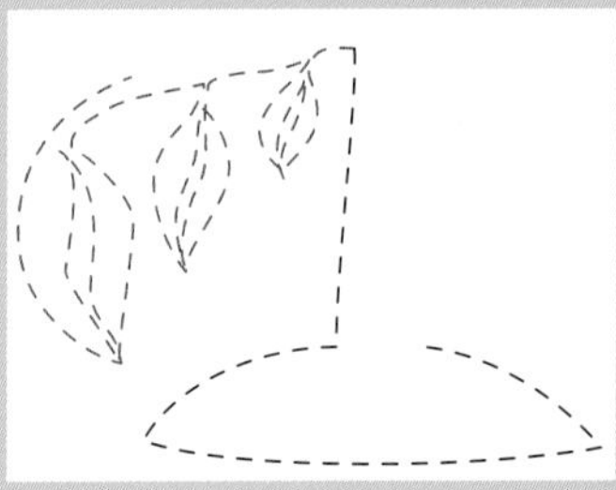

3
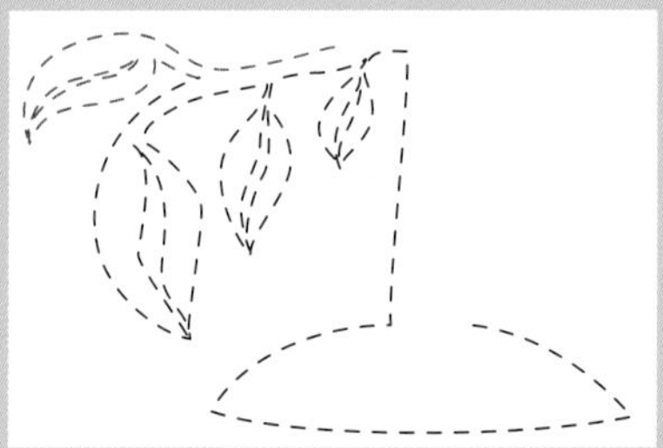

4
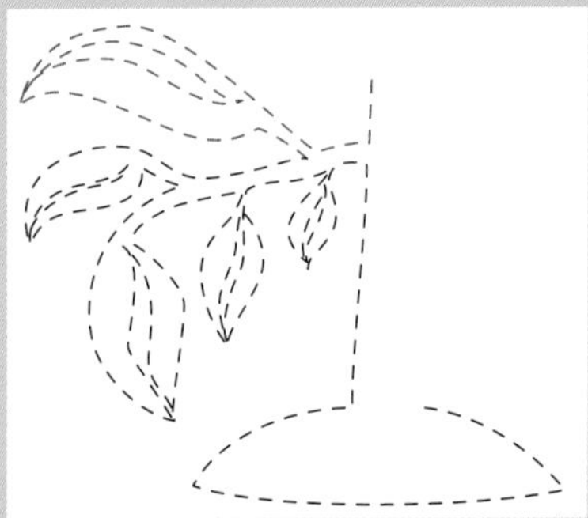

5

6

7

8

9

10

Willow Leaf Formation

Sample shapes for willow leaves

Willow Tree with Guidelines for Branches

1

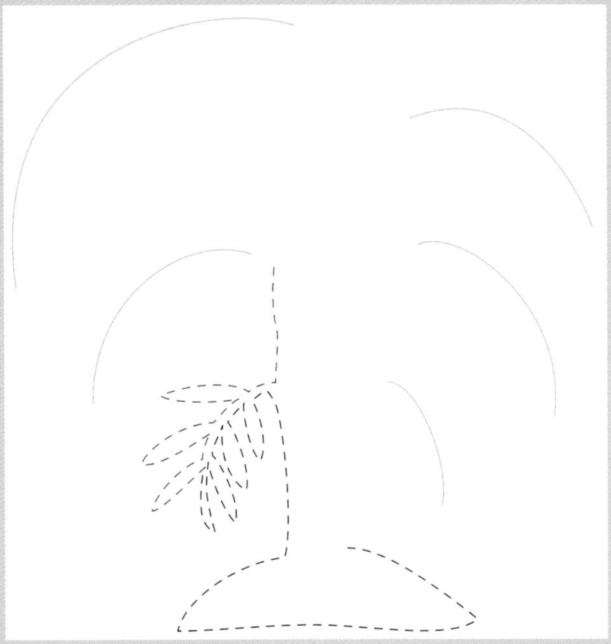

2

Willow Tree Quilts

Willow Tree Quilt 1, cottons, unknown maker, Eastern United States, c. 1815–1825, 84″ × 86″

Willow Tree Quilt 2, cottons, unknown maker, Eastern United States, c. 1815–1825, 78″ × 92″

Detail view of stuffed work, Willow Tree Quilt 1

Stuffed work sometimes enhanced the quilting in early wholecloth quilts, especially all white quilts made of cottons. The technique, known to some today as trapunto, involved stuffing cotton wadding and cords inside quilted motifs to give them extra loft. Often done through small incisions on the back of the quilt, stuffed work created a three-dimensional effect.

Whitework was an ideal expression of neoclassicism. The all-white quilts with raised relief resembled the marble carvings in ancient sculpture and architecture. The Willow Tree Quilts were part of that tradition. Both quilts came from an estate in Duxbury, Massachusetts, originally purchased from a dealer in New Jersey. They were auctioned at separate times but ultimately remained together.

Both quilts include a variety of botanical motifs surrounding a large, central willow tree. Many of the motifs are seen in both quilts, but the fabric, composition, and finishing differed. The differences could suggest more than one maker or date of origin, but the similarities were truly remarkable.

Oval Chain

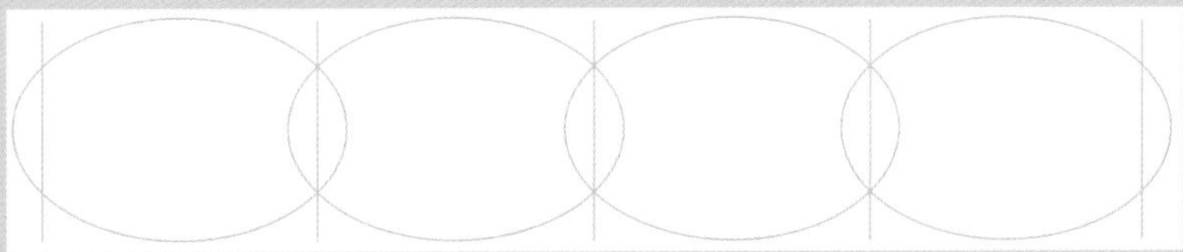

1

2

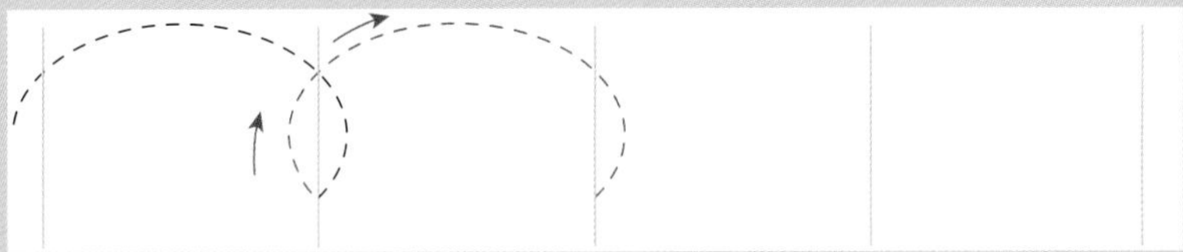

3

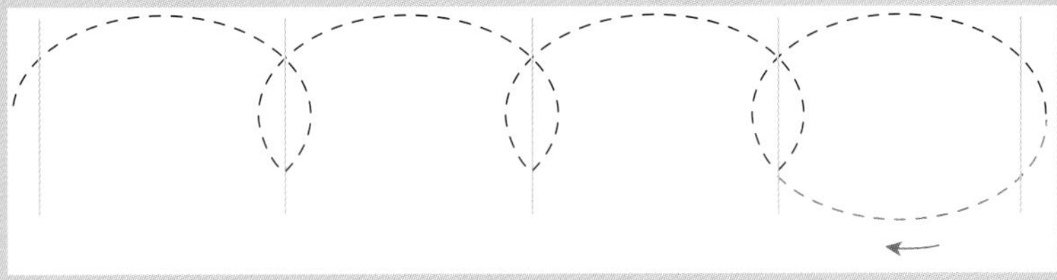

4

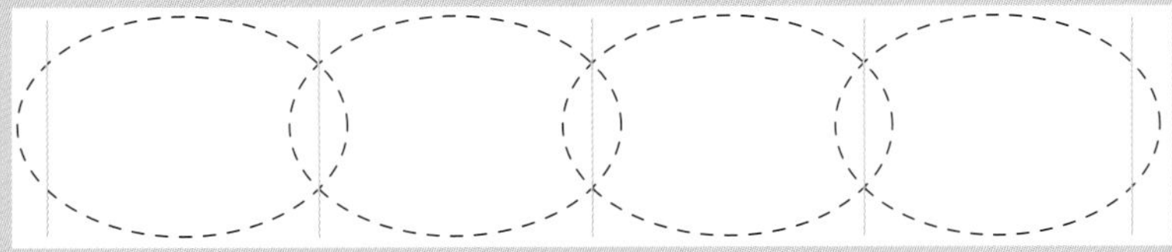

5

note

The oval curves for this chain are ideal for borders and sashing, as they are used in the original quilt. For the most consistent shape, you may find it beneficial to use an oval-shaped acrylic template and ruler foot for your machine. Please consult your machine manufacturer to determine if your machine is capable of ruler work and if there are specific requirements.

Willow Tree with Broken Stump

1

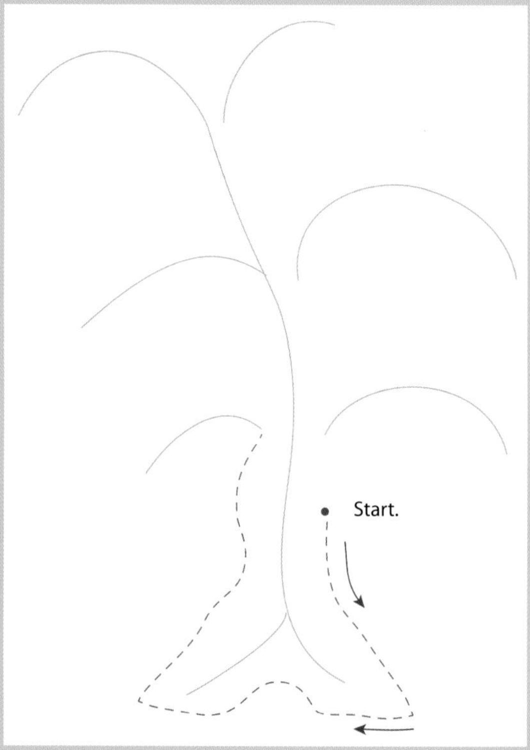

Sketch graceful shape and then stitch trunk.

2

3

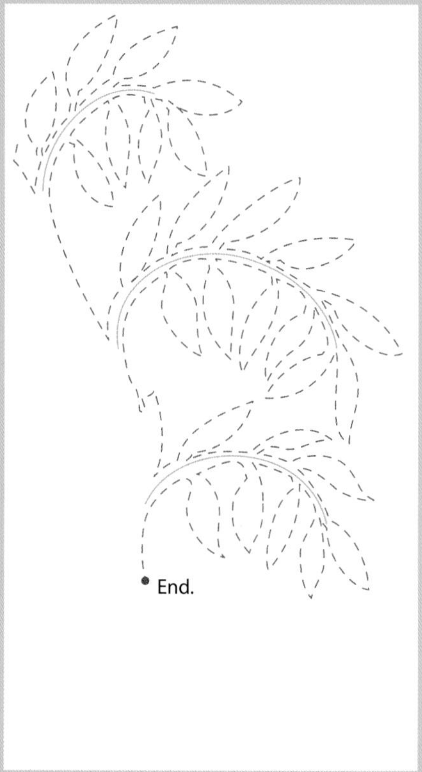

Palm Leaf

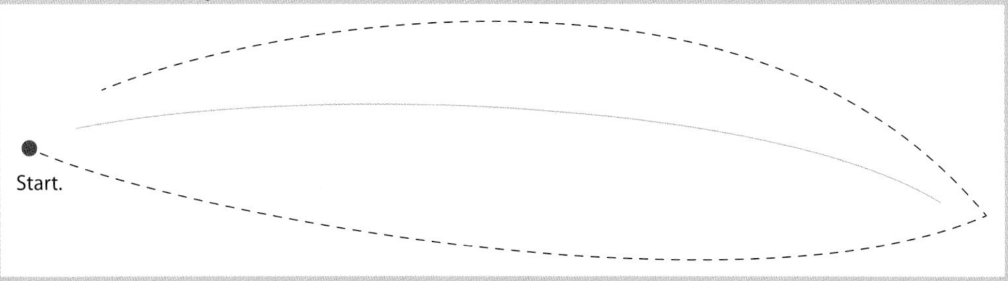

1

Sketch spine, stitch shapes using gentle curves, pointed tip, and open base.

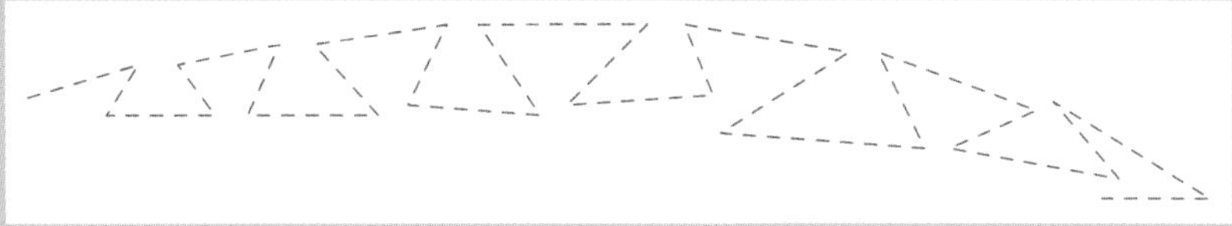

2

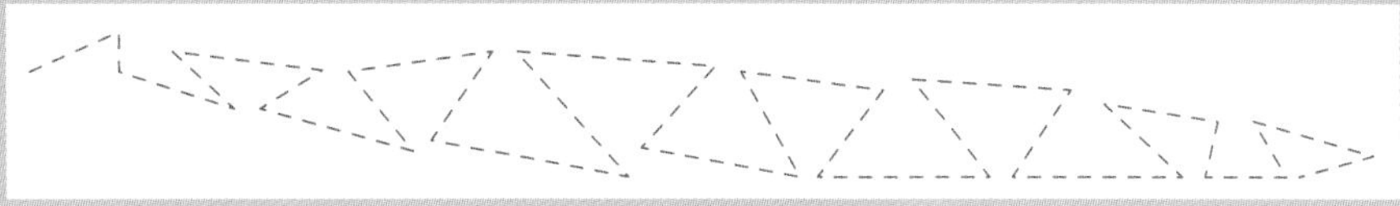

3

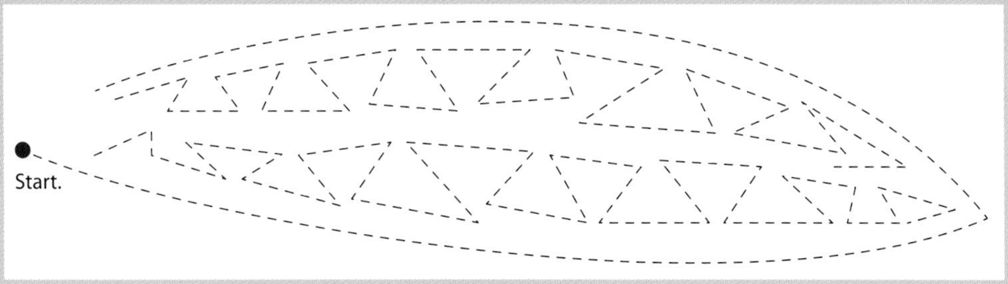

4

Palm Tree

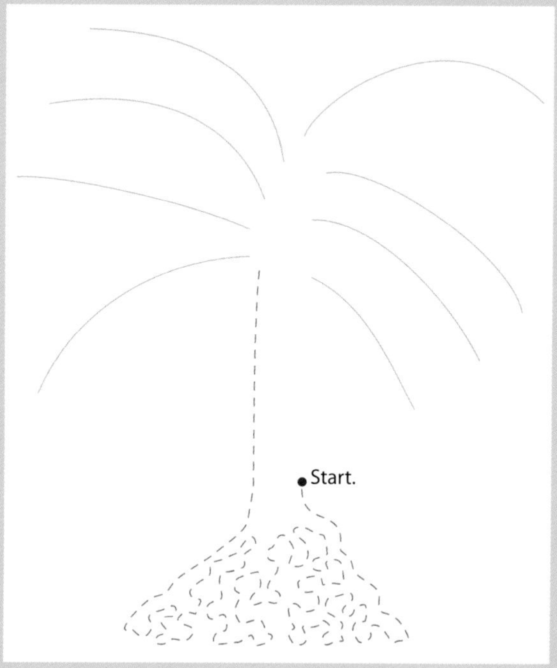

1

Use stippling technique for roots. Pick general area and go to town. Sketch out shape of leaves.

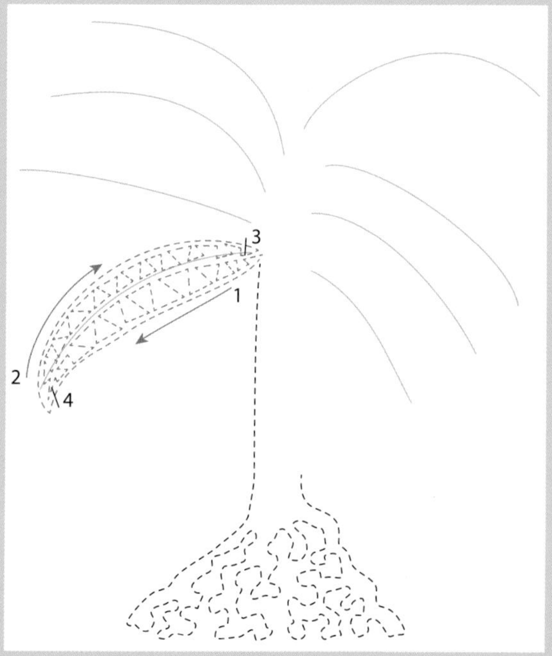

2

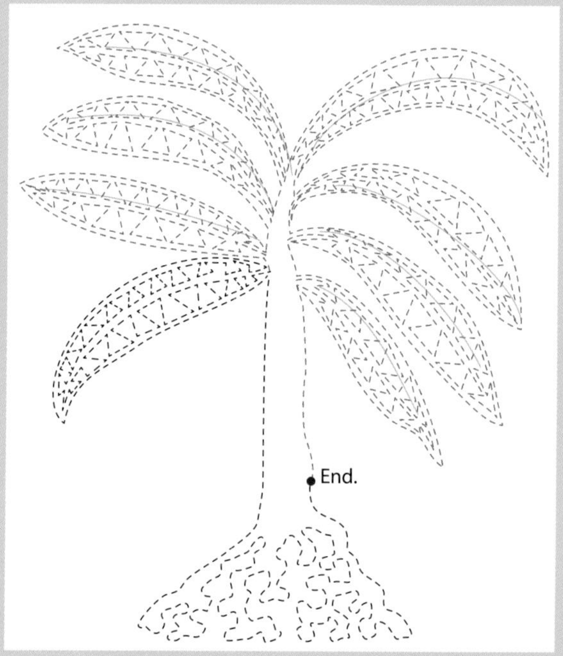

3

Oak Leaf

1

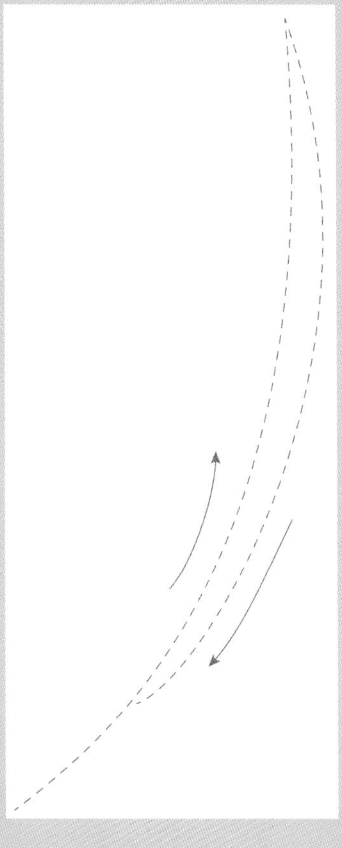

2

Oak Tree

1

Sketch graceful shape, and then stitch trunk using any shape you like for base.

2

Bell Flowers

1

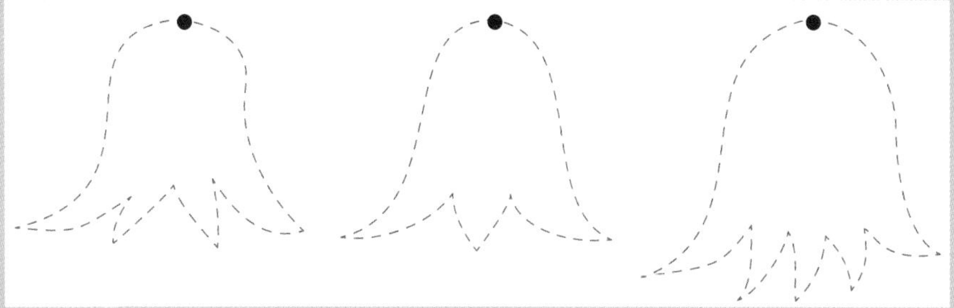

Start and end at same spot. Petal points vary in number. Other bell-like flower shapes may be used.

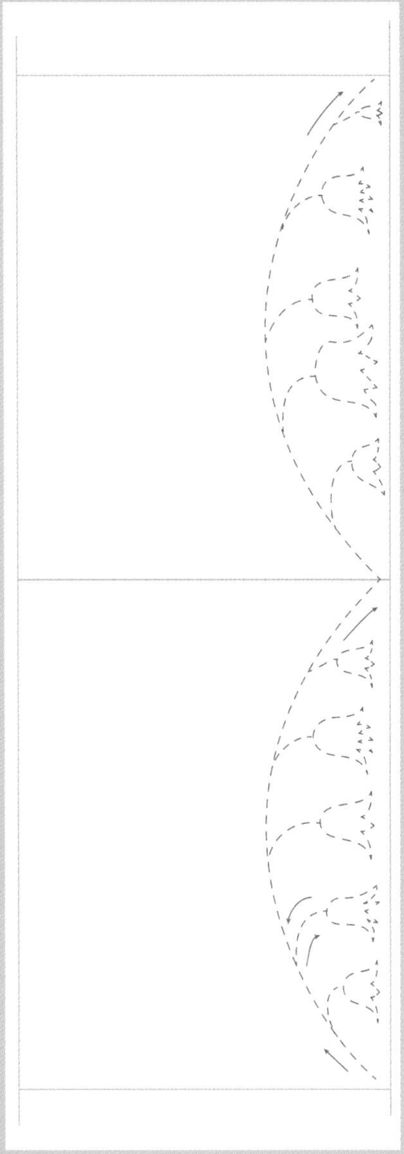

2

3

Swag

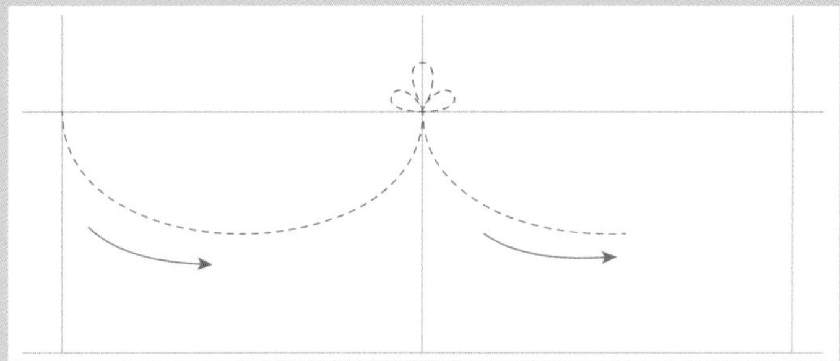

1

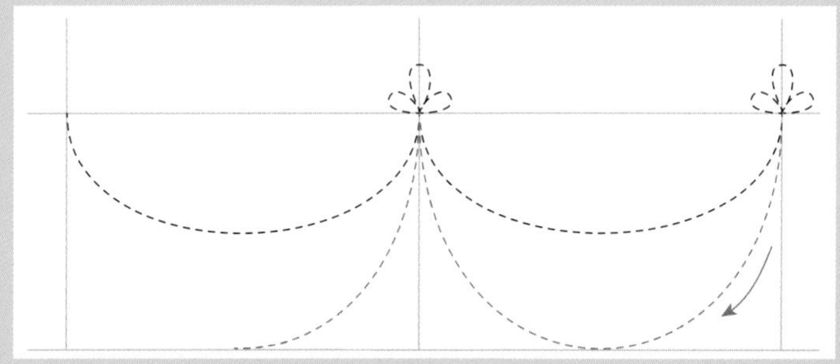

2

Large Peony

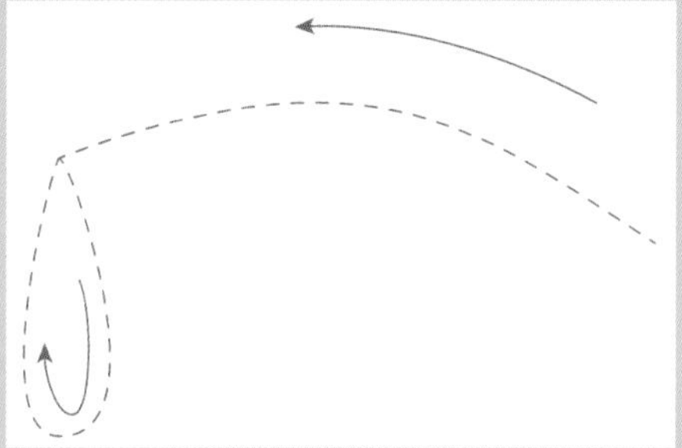

1

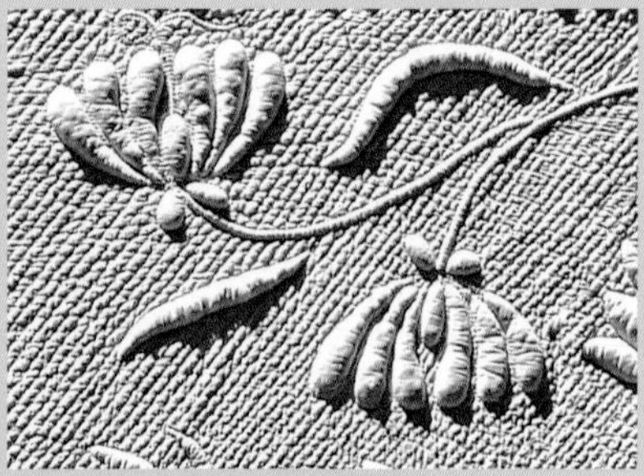

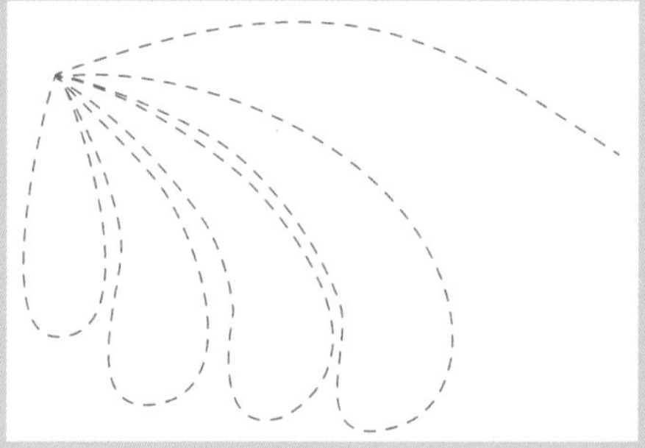

2

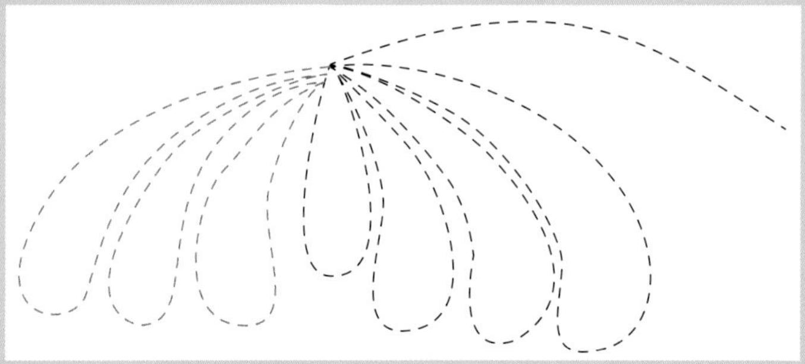

3

Aster

Small Peony

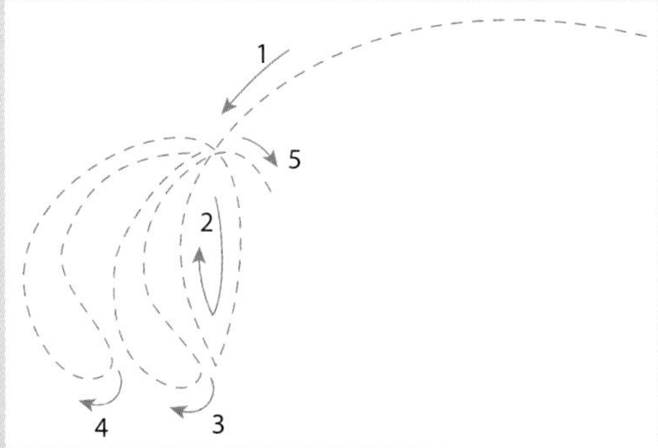

1

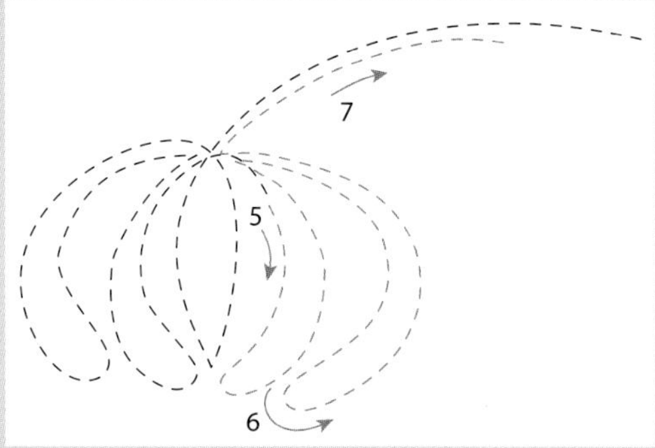

2

Album with Lyre Quilt

Album with Lyre Quilt, cottons, made by Mary Couchman Small, Martinsburg, Berkeley County, West Virginia c. 1850, 93″ × 93″

Block details of Album with Lyre Quilt

Made in the style of a Baltimore Album quilt, this masterpiece album with Lyre was made in West Virginia. Some quilts demonstrated more creativity in the patchwork than the quilting, and that was often the case with elaborate appliqué quilts made in the Baltimore Album style. These quilts were generally made around the middle nineteenth century in Baltimore and surrounding areas, but also migrated and evolved.

Block details of Album with Lyre Quilt

Martinsburg, West Virginia, was about 100 miles west of Baltimore, but the Small family made quilts in the Baltimore Album style. Mary Couchman Small made this magnificent album quilt, likely with the help of her daughters. One of her daughters, Harriet, was attributed as the maker of an almost identical quilt documented by the West Virginia Heritage Quilt Search.

The appliqué designs were folksy interpretations of the motifs seen in Baltimore Album quilts, and included pots of flowers, wreaths with fruits and hearts, and a lyre in the center. The whimsical appliqué designs were made with a limited palette of four fabrics, surrounded by extremely dense echo quilting, all done by hand.

The continuous-line quilting designs presented are a sampling of what you can do when converting appliqué shapes to quilting motifs. The baskets in each corner offer a huge variety of shapes and combinations, and are a great source of inspiration to mix and match and create your own designs.

Lily Variation

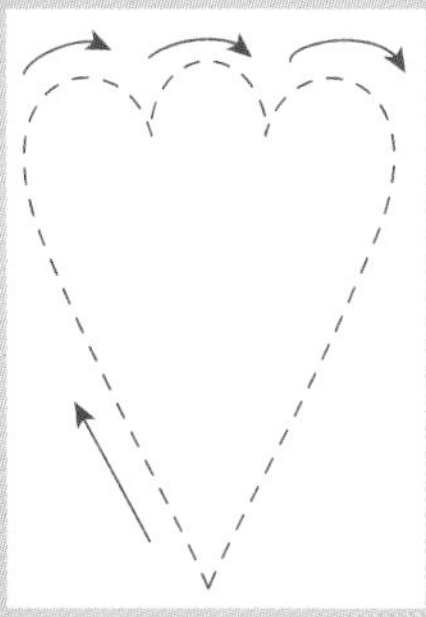
1

2

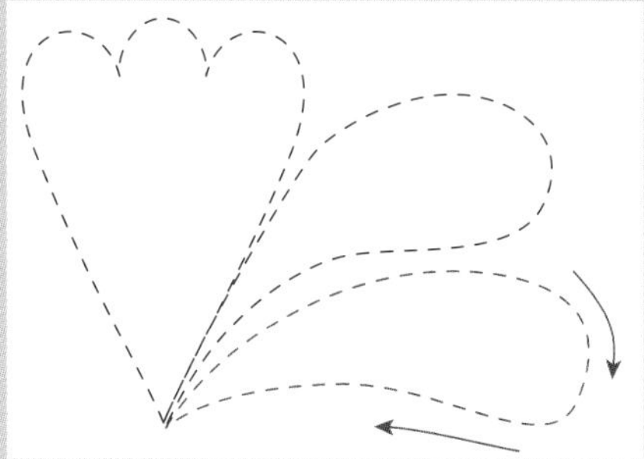
3

4

5

Lily with variation to bottom leaf

Stacked Heart Medallion

This wonderful heart design is easy to do with a single pattern (see Heart-Shaped Medallions, page 126). Enlarge the pattern to the desired size (Mandy likes to think of it in terms of circumference, and imagine it fitting inside a circle), and trace onto card stock or template plastic. Using the marking tool of your choice, trace one side, as below. Then, flip the pattern over, line the points up, and trace the mirror side. It may be helpful to mark a circle divided into eight wedges to help lay out your pattern. Once your center medallion is done, surround it with a heart wreath for a truly standout combination.

1

2

3

4

5

6

Pearls and Pebbles

Small circles, either as a fill known as pebbles or a chain known as pearls are a useful tool for quilters. They can be used in a variety of ways, either on their own or combined with other elements to make a more complex design.

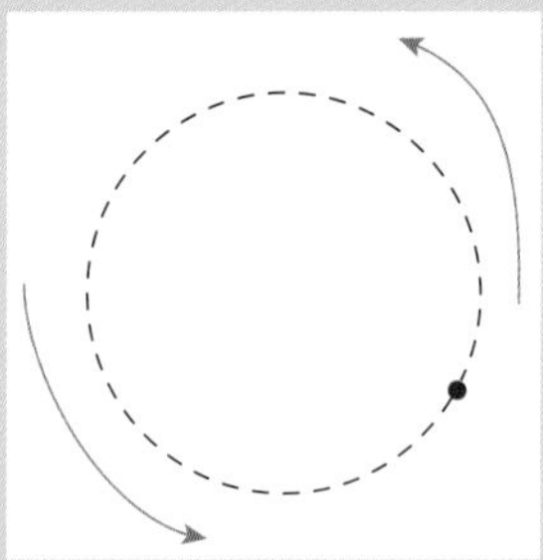

1

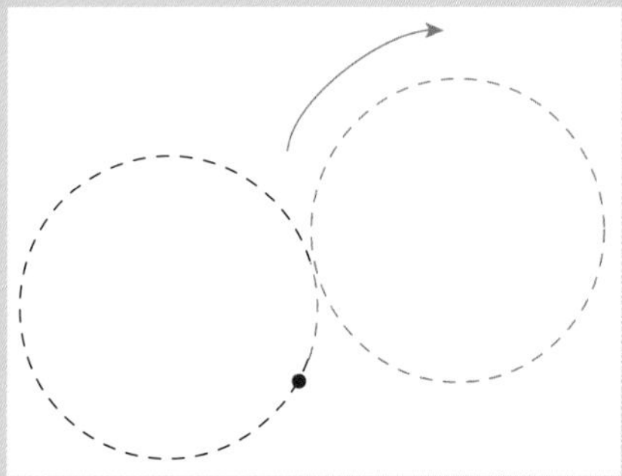

2

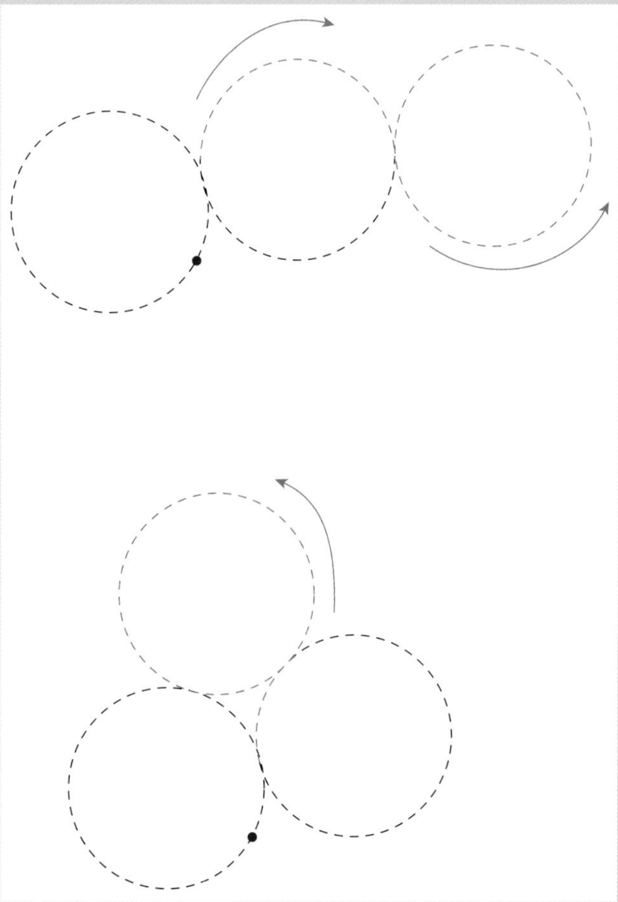

3

Haws

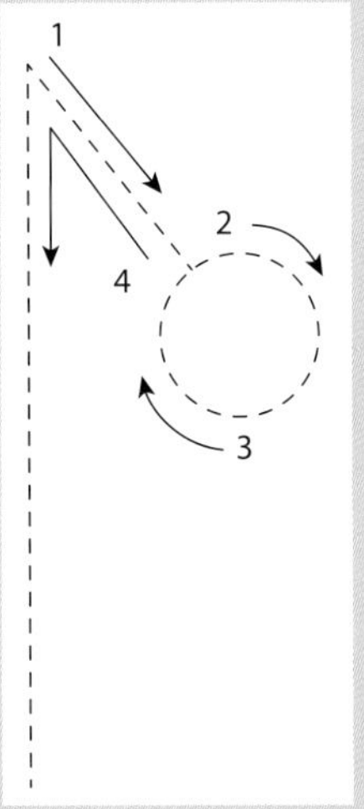

1

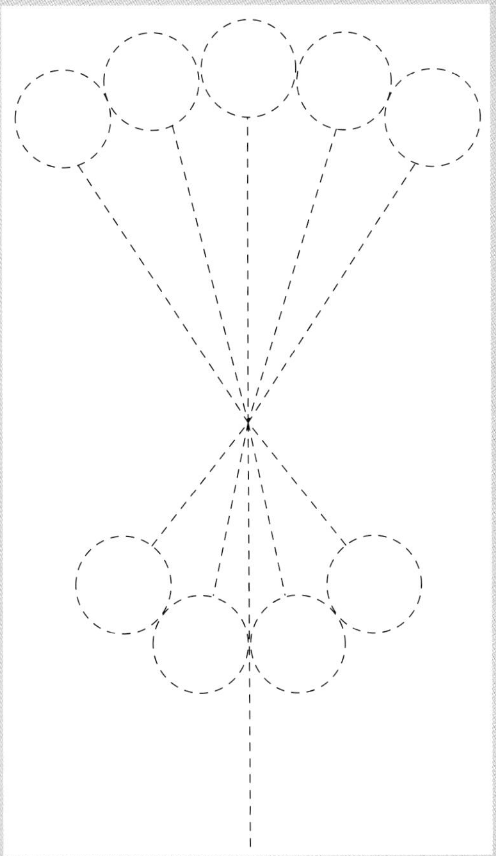

2

Holly Leaf Formation

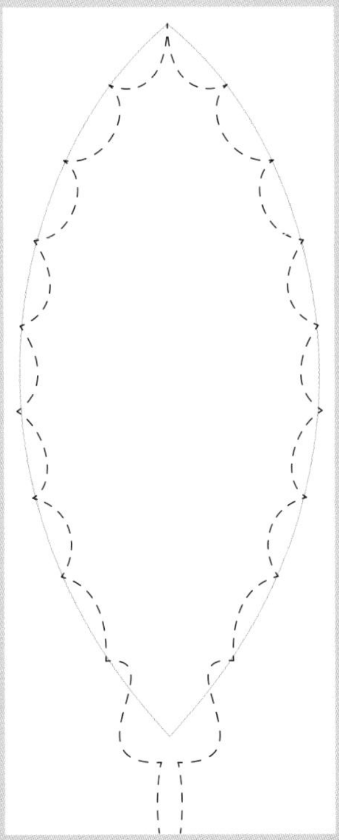

Holly Medallion

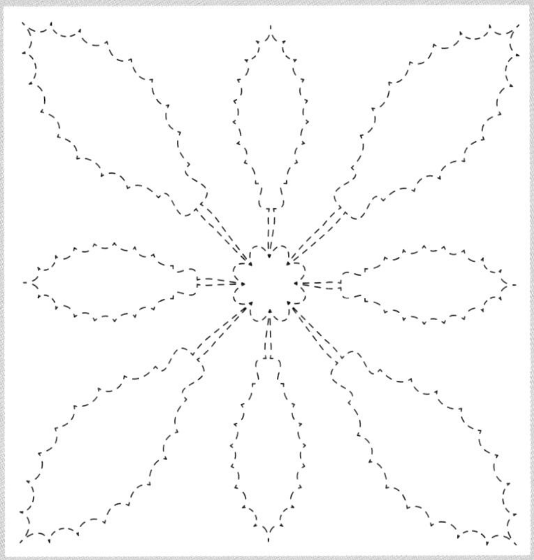

Pomegranate

1
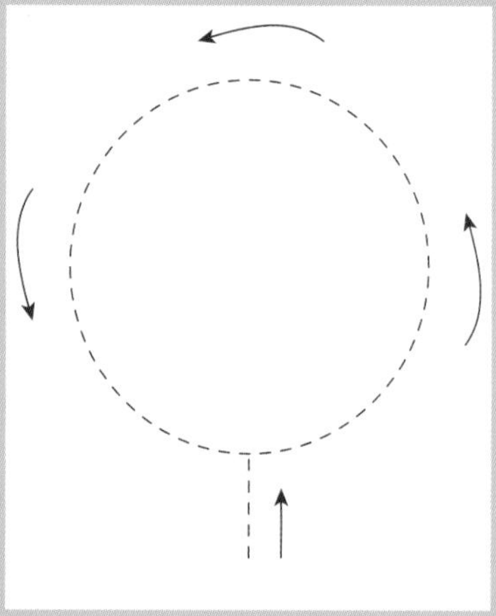

2
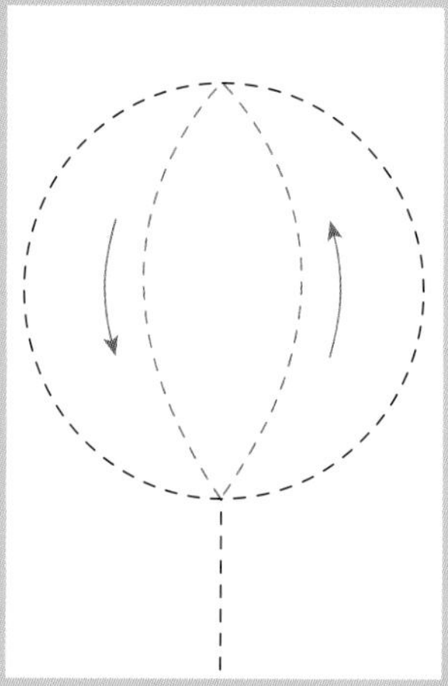

3
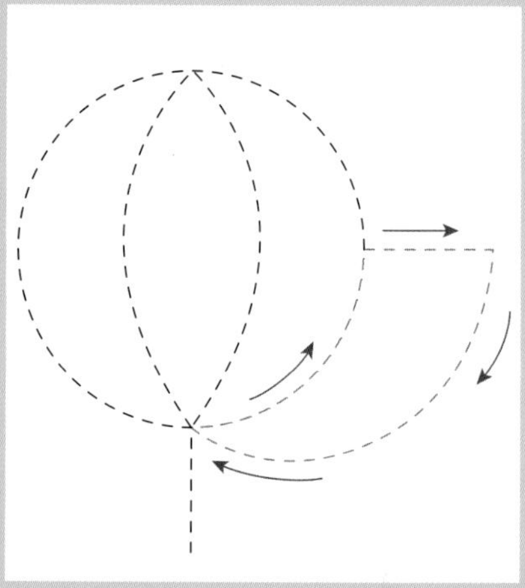

4
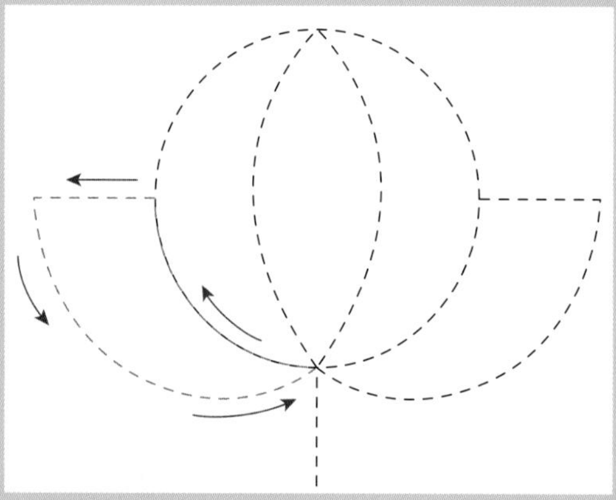

5
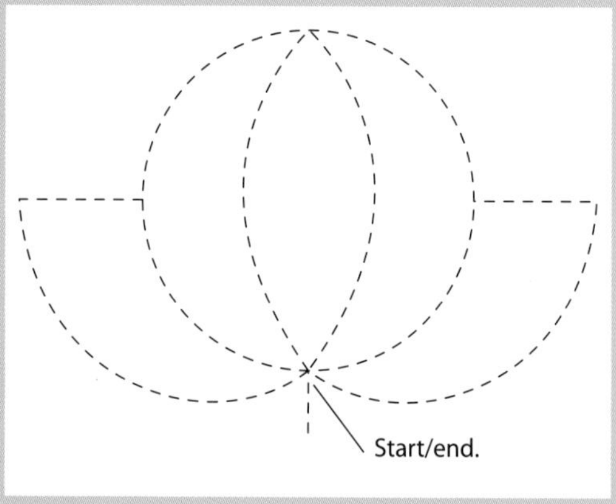

Pomegranate Wreath

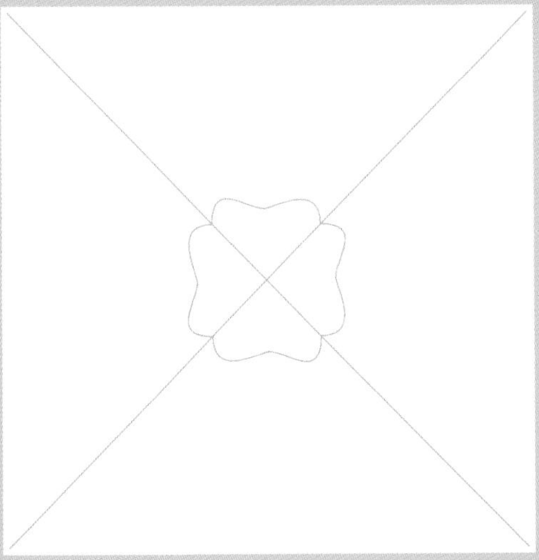

1

2

Coxscomb Flower Head

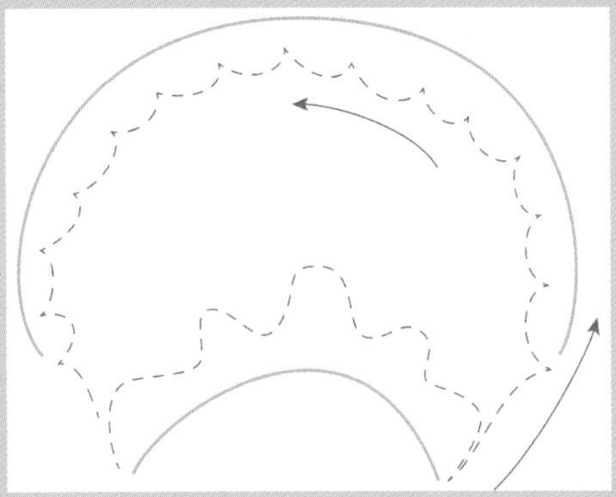

1

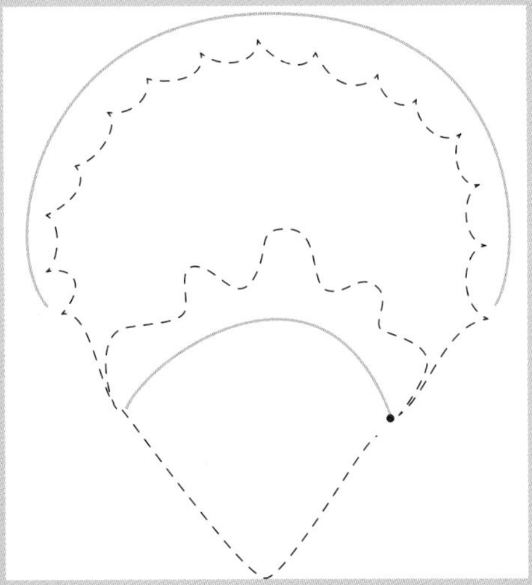

2

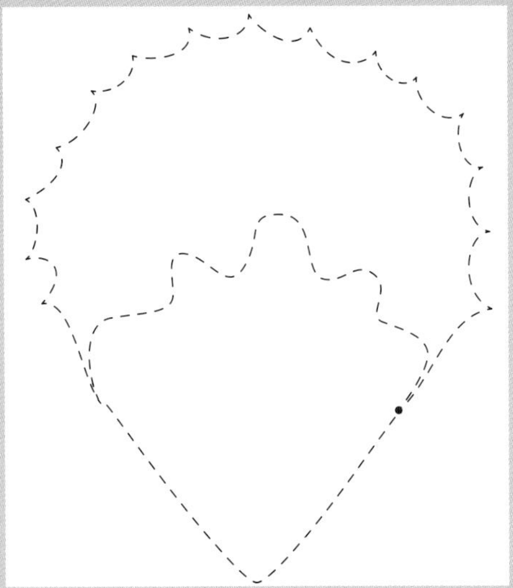

3

Thistle Flower

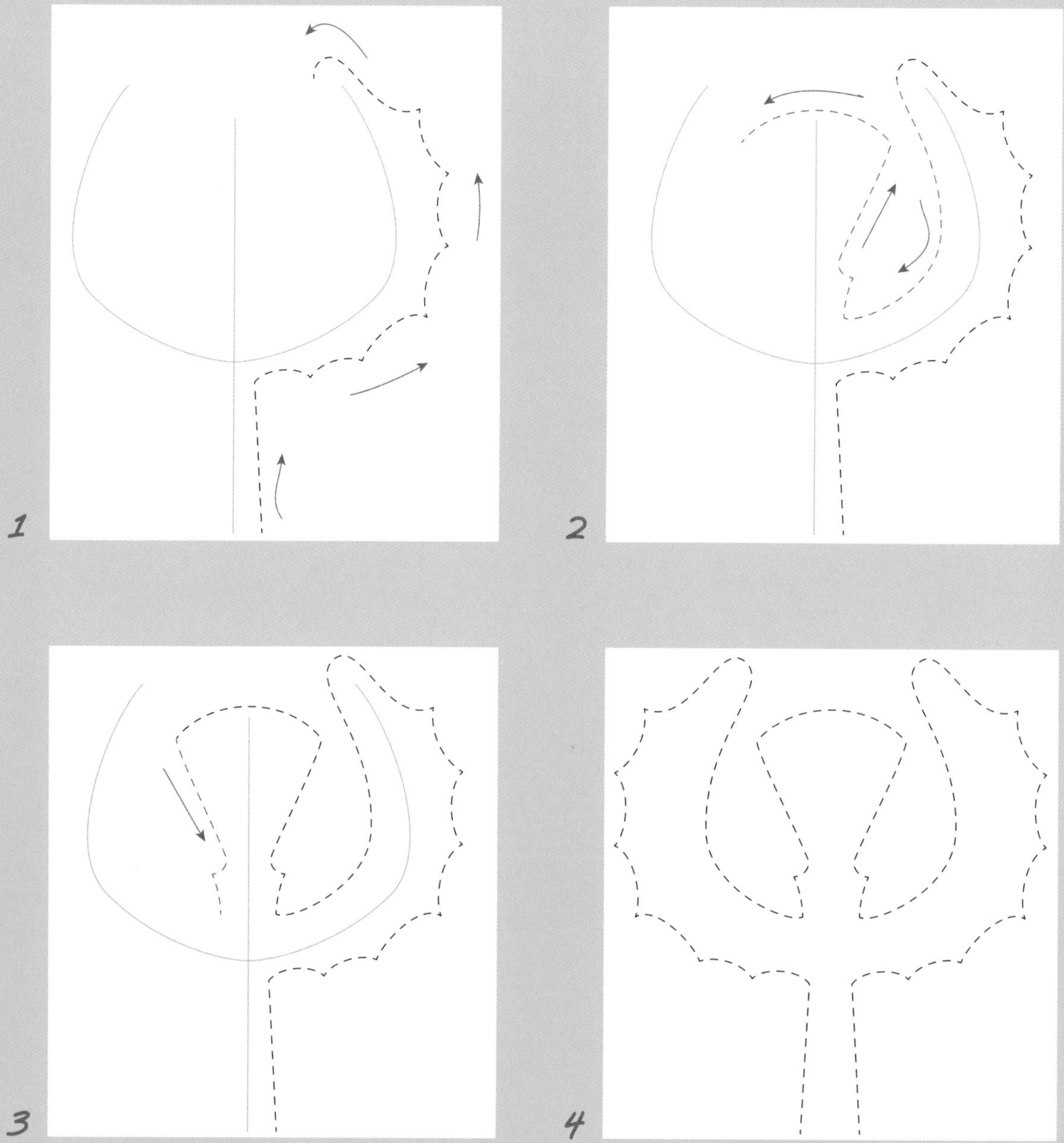

Thistle Basket

1

Basket is deliberately petite, approximately one-third of the total height.

2

Simple Basket

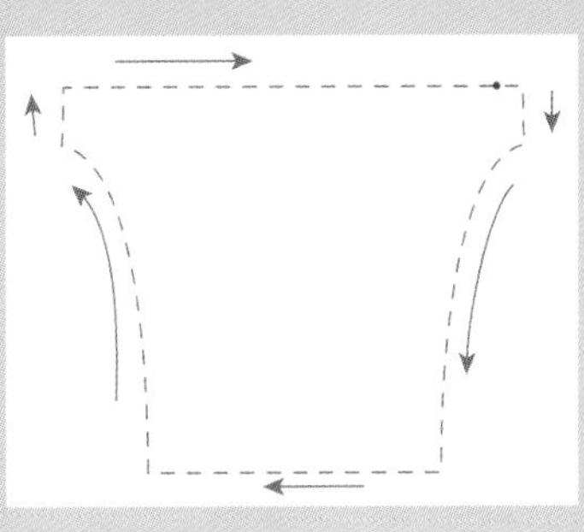

1

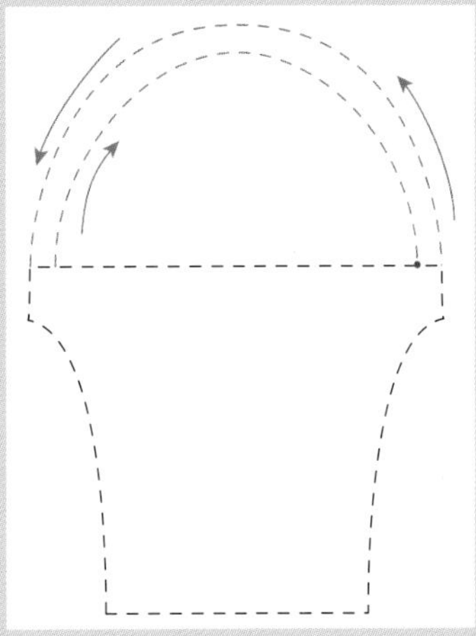

2

Basket 1

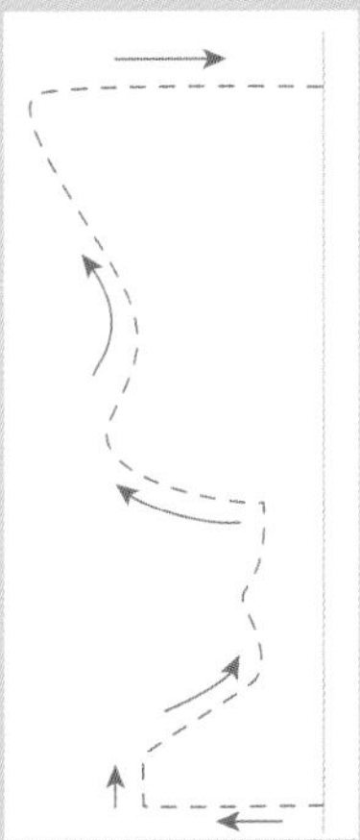

1

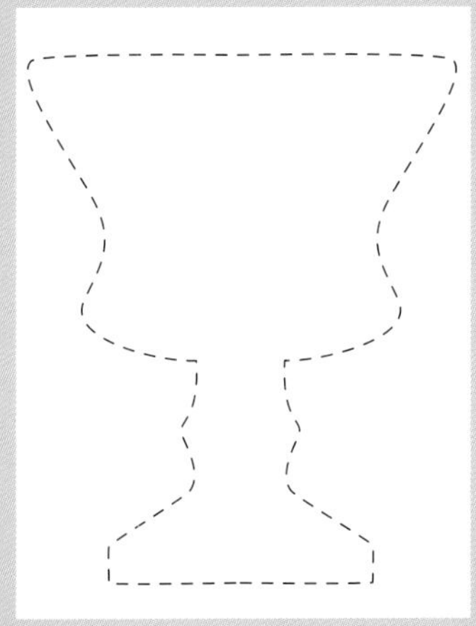

2

Basket 2

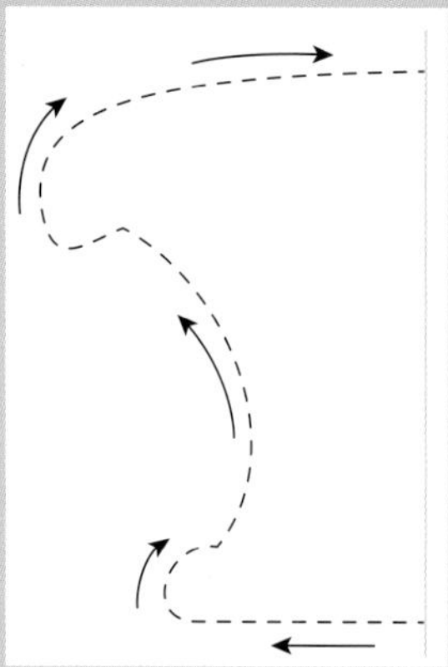
1

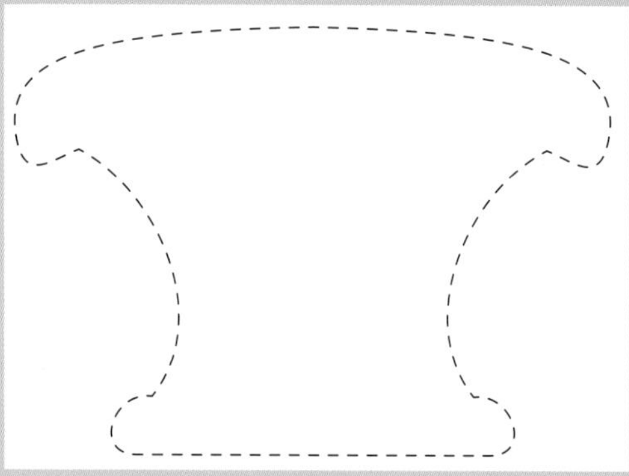
2

Pear

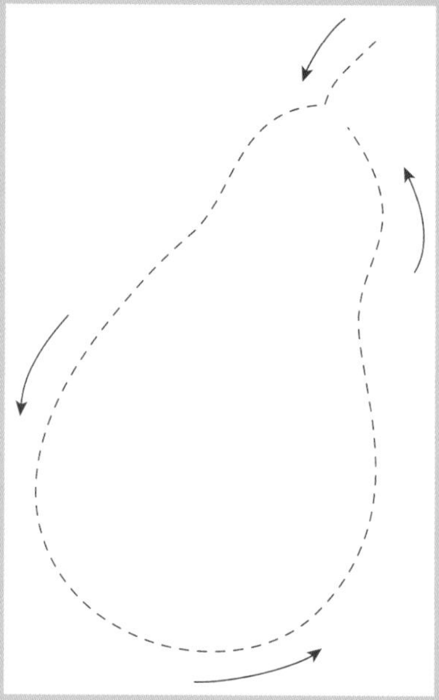

Apple

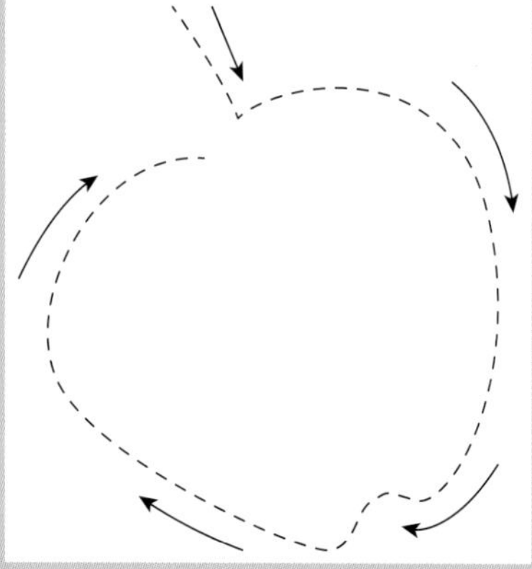

Plum

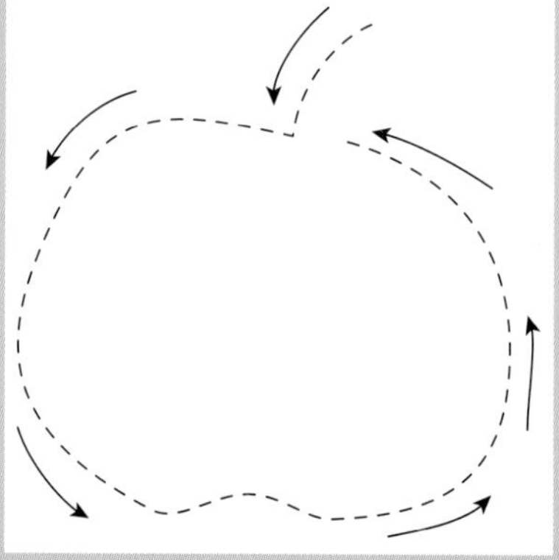
Alternate arrangement

Apple and Pear Wreath

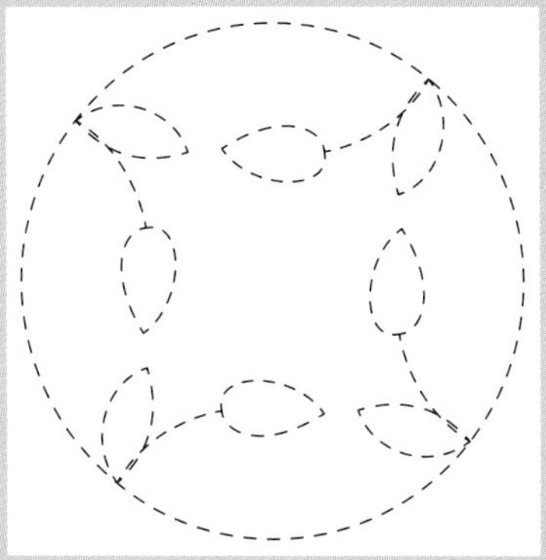

1

2

3

Simple Heart Medallion

1

2

Rose Wreath

1

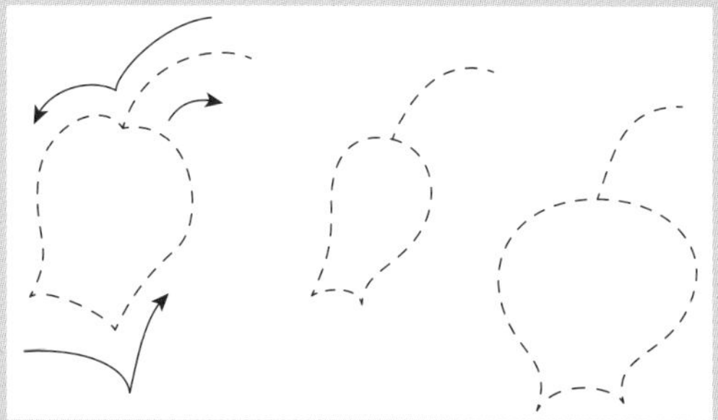

Mandy likes to sketch out the stems with a marking tool to make sure they are balanced.

2

3

Four-Block Appliqué Quilt

Four-Block Appliqué Quilt, cottons, unknown maker, Eastern United States, found in Oregon, c. 1850, 73″ × 73″

In the middle nineteenth century, elegant appliqué quilts made of predominately red and green on a white ground were quite popular. Four-block quilts were among the familiar forms. Within the genre, some designs were more unusual than others. Fanciful pots of flowers were not uncommon, but some designs were less common than others.

This 1850s four-block appliqué quilt is unusual. It is a rescue quilt, in poor condition but very much worth preserving because of its original, whimsical designs. Bill found the quilt in an antique shop in Portland and sent it to Mandy. She was enthralled, particularly with the quilting motifs and how they all fit together like the pieces of a puzzle.

If you ever find a quilt in poor condition and there is something interesting or unusual about it, rescue it! The effort to draft the designs and make new quilts is certainly worth it.

Mandy found the quilting to be an interesting blend of stand-alone motifs that mimic the appliqué and quilting elements that combined with the appliqué to form a cohesive unit. The quilting element that ties these two techniques together is *echo quilting*, which is when the quilter lays down a line of stitching that follows a shape one or more times. Sometimes echo quilting is used to fill an entire block or quilt.

Appliquéd Leaf with Echoed Detail

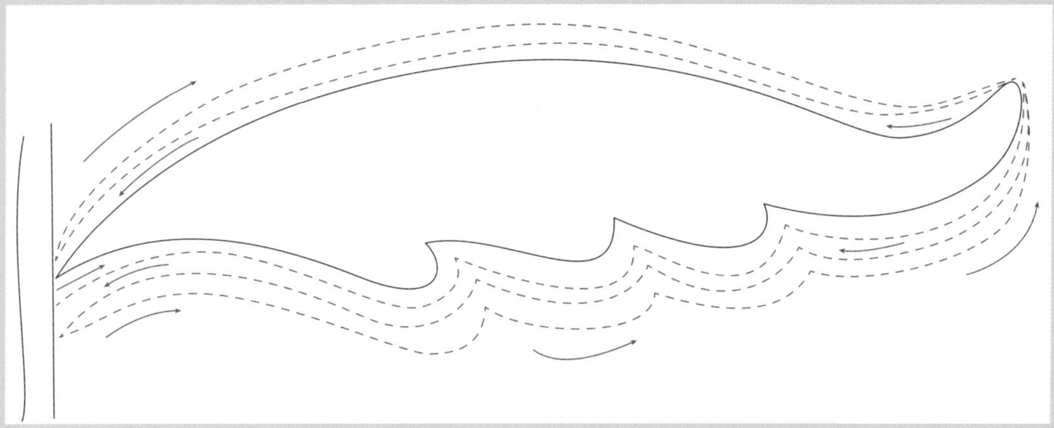

1

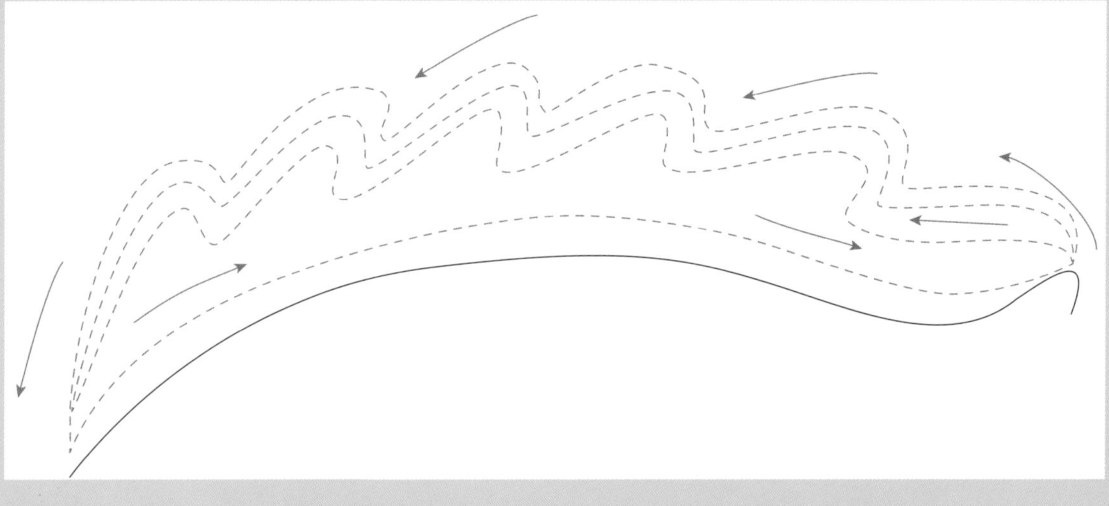

2

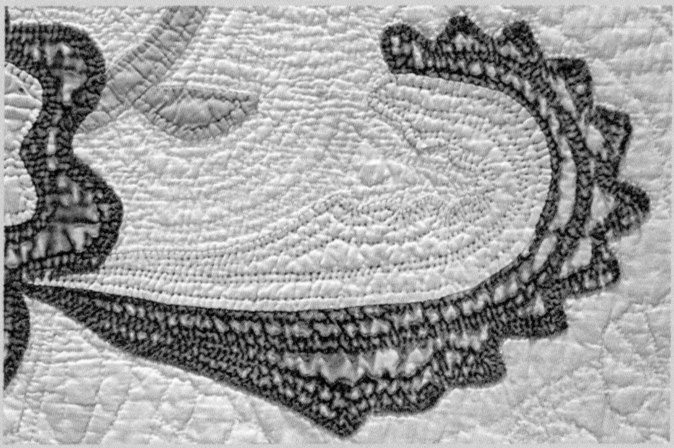

Bowl with Echoed Detail

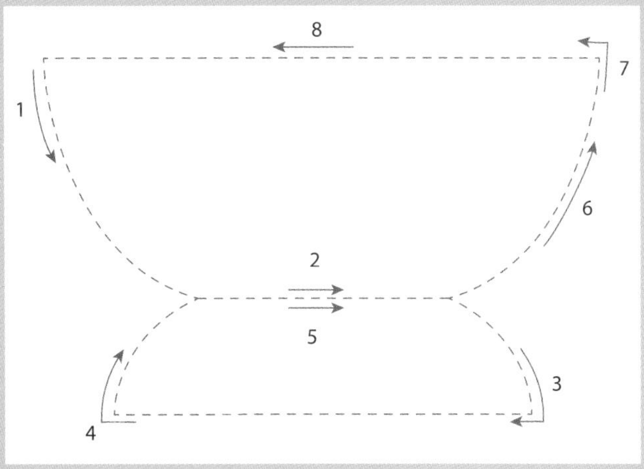

1

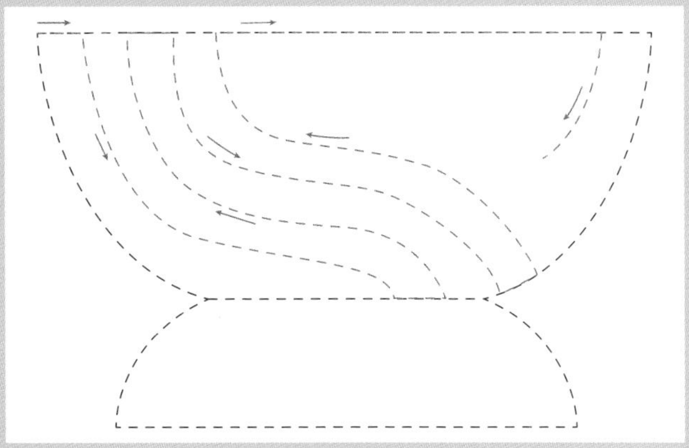

2

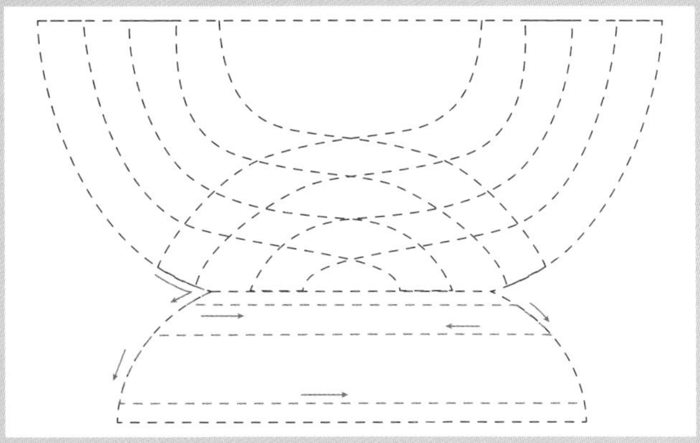

3

Heart-Shaped Feathers

Sometimes the way you form a flower can change the overall look. Mandy will use this when she wants her petal tips to look a little boxier rather than a teardrop shape: Make a stem into the center (you may wish to draw in guidelines. Mandy prefers to start with eight arms, including the stem, then subdivide into sixteen arms). From the center, stitch out and backtrack to almost the center, and repeat for each arm. Try to avoid going exactly to the center, or you will have an unsightly thread buildup! Once you come back to the center, bounce around the outside, forming your boxy petals. The extra-thick rays also change the look of the flower.

1

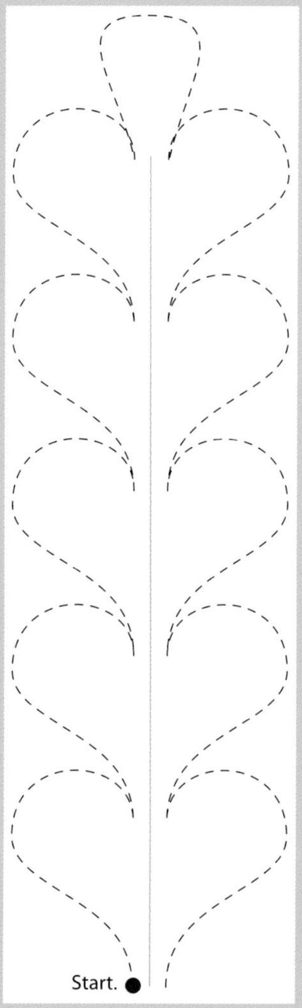

2

Posey

1

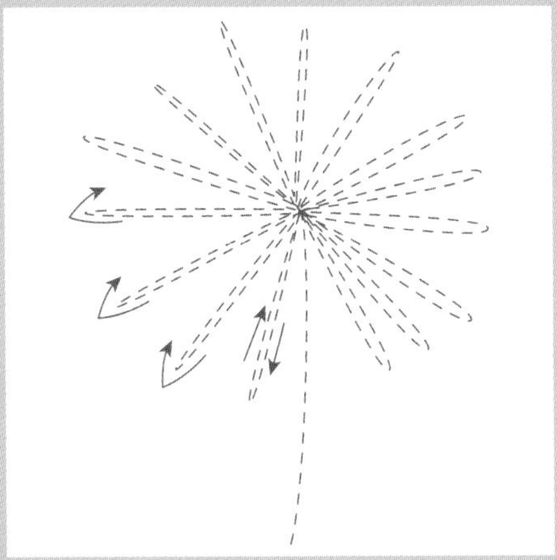

2

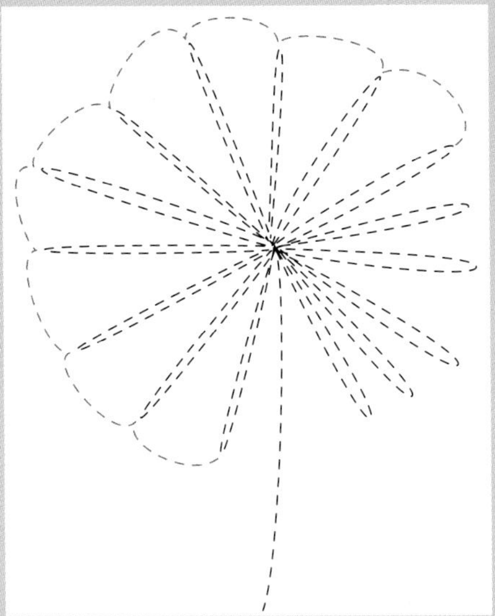

3

Combining the Elements

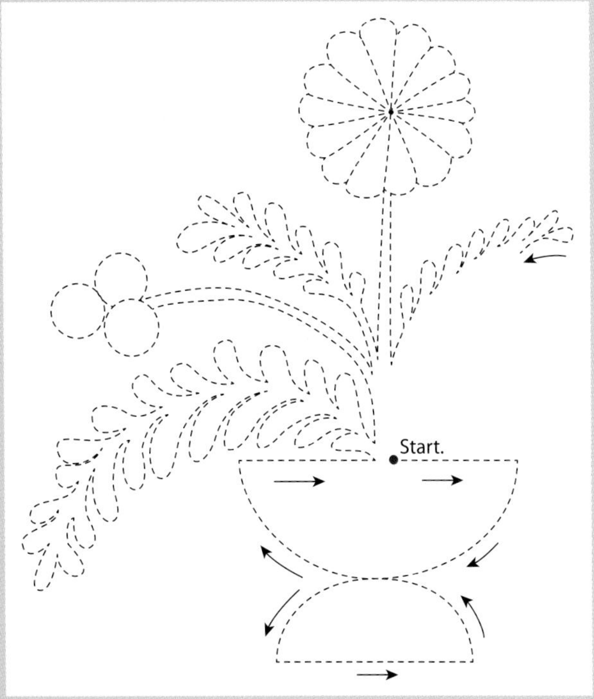

Appliqué Sampler WITH WREATHS AND BIRDS QUILT

Appliqué Sampler with Wreaths and Birds Quilt, cottons, unknown maker, Pennsylvania, c. 1870, 74″ × 91″

Appliqué quilts remained popular long after the period of Baltimore Album quilts in the 1840s and 1850s. As the form evolved, quiltmakers experimented with new designs and new interpretations of old designs. Botanical elements were still among the most popular motifs, but there were plenty of others.

This appliqué sampler with wreaths and birds is surprisingly modern in its streamlined approach. Compared to other examples of the period, the motifs are sparse looking, almost like stick-figure representations of the earlier designs.

It is also unusual in its use of narrow, bias-cut appliqué. Quiltmakers today will sometimes use bias-cut appliqué, and when people recently introduced the technique it appeared to be a twenty-first-century idea. It wasn't. Someone tried it almost 150 years ago. That's the great thing about old quilts. They have so many ideas.

The continuous-line quilting motifs derived from these appliqué designs are really fantastic variations of grids. While many of them have flowers incorporated, it would be very easy to use the grids alone, either as a background fill or a stand-alone design. You may also find it simpler to purchase a large stencil with precut diagonal lines rather than drawing your own each time!

Single Diagonal Crosshatch

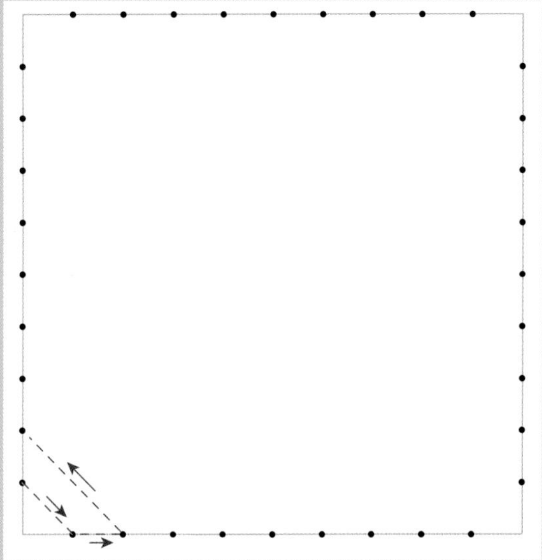

Single Crosshatch

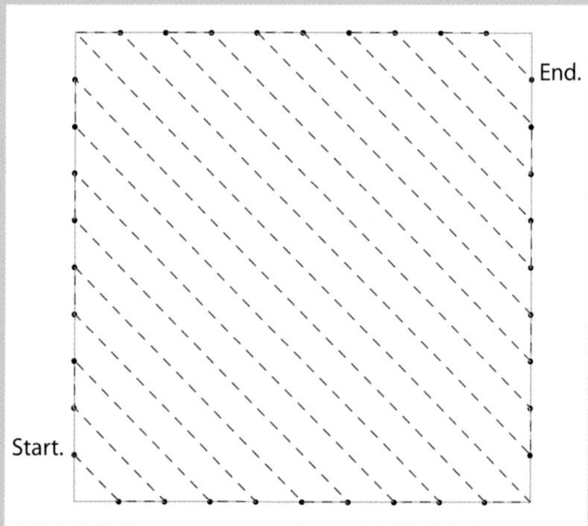

1

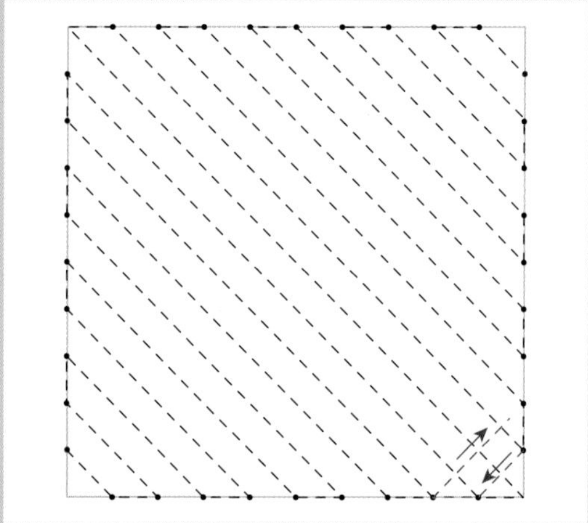

2

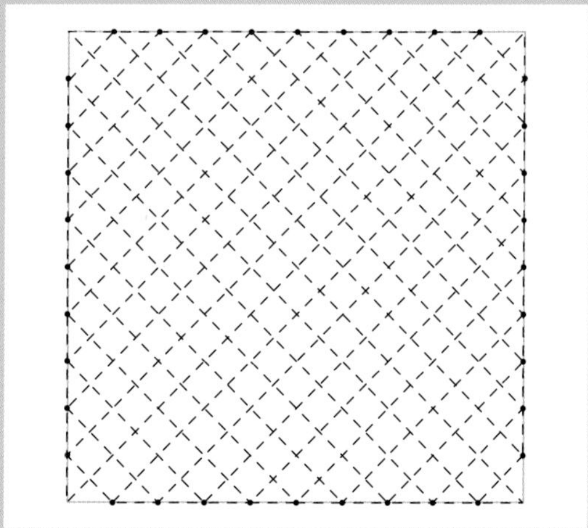

3

Echoed Single Hatch

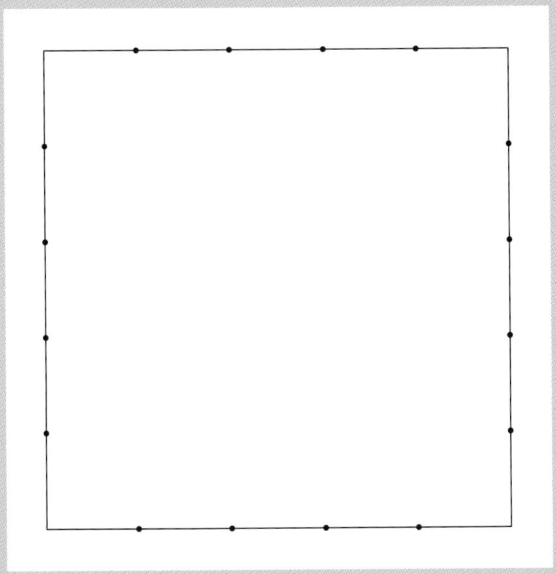

1

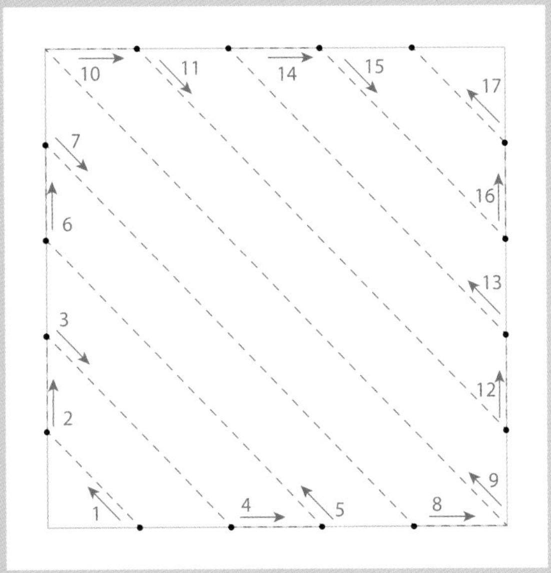

2

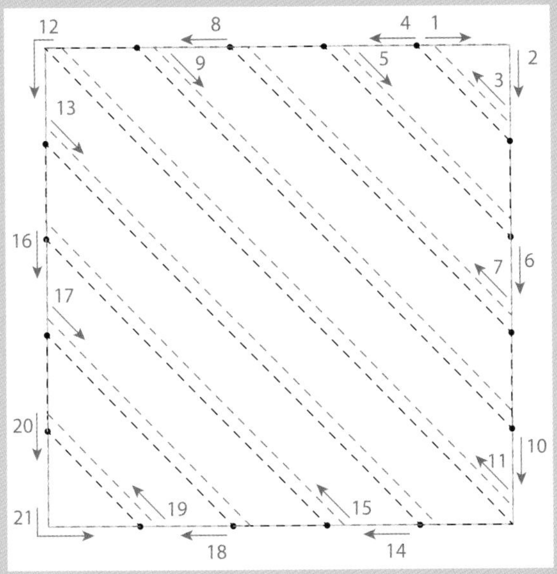

3

Echoed Crosshatch

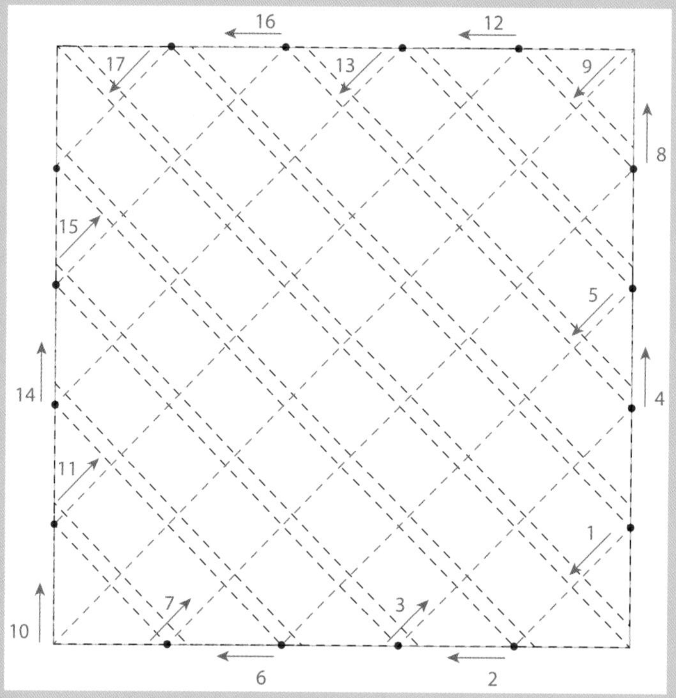

1

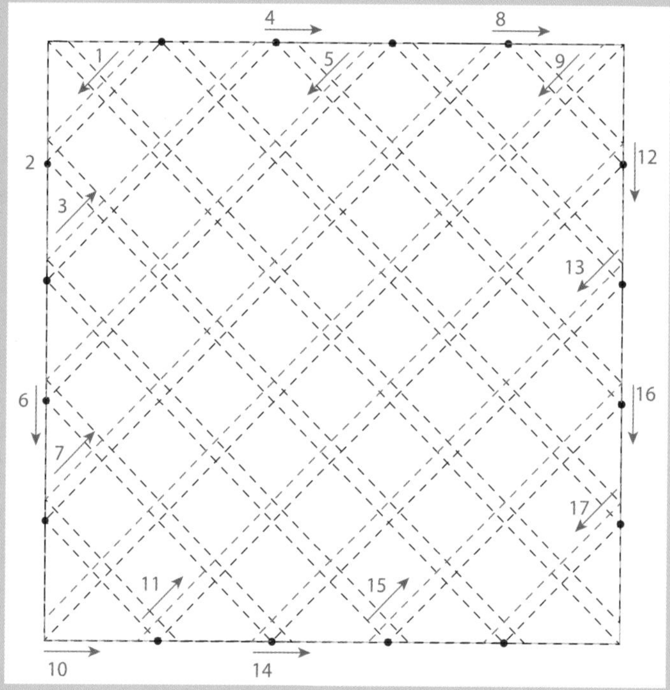

2

Plaid Grid

1

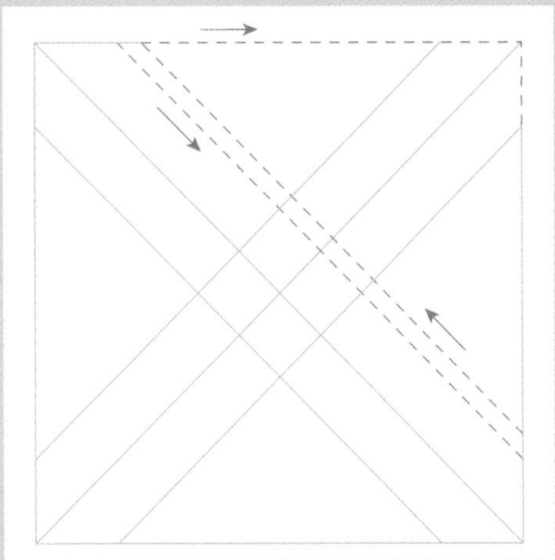

2

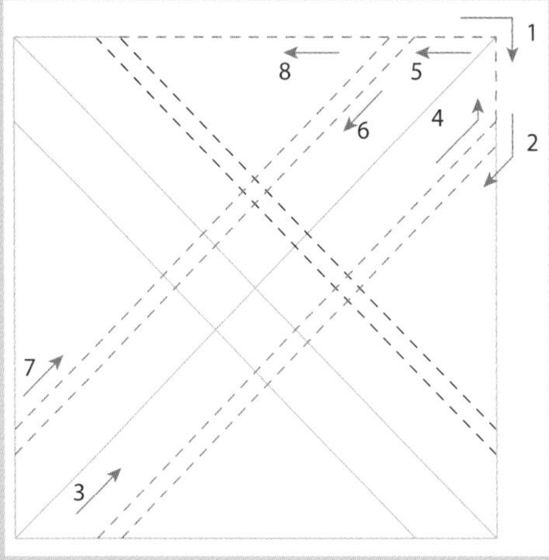

3

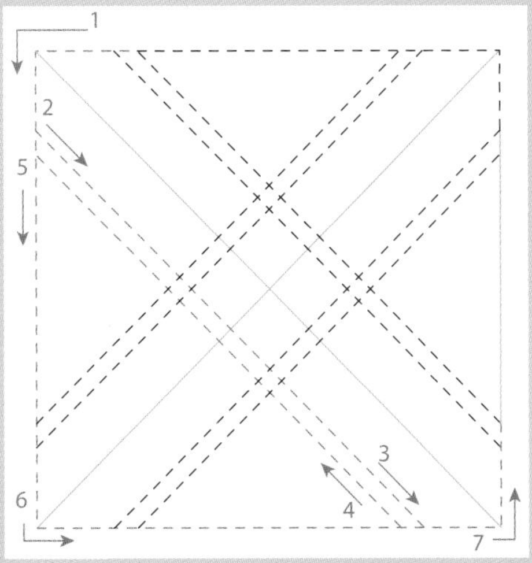

4

5

Off-Center Grid

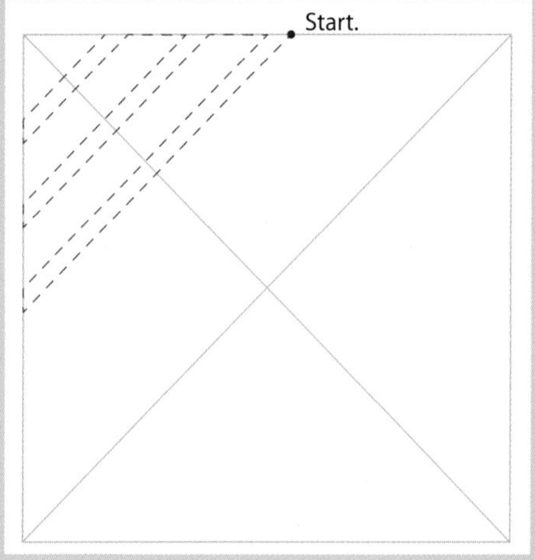

1

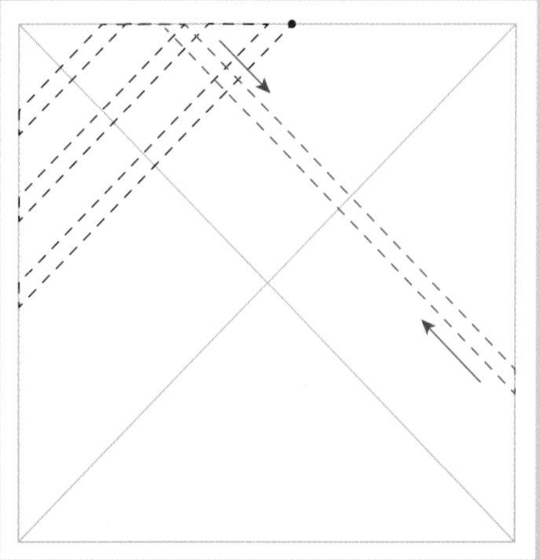

2

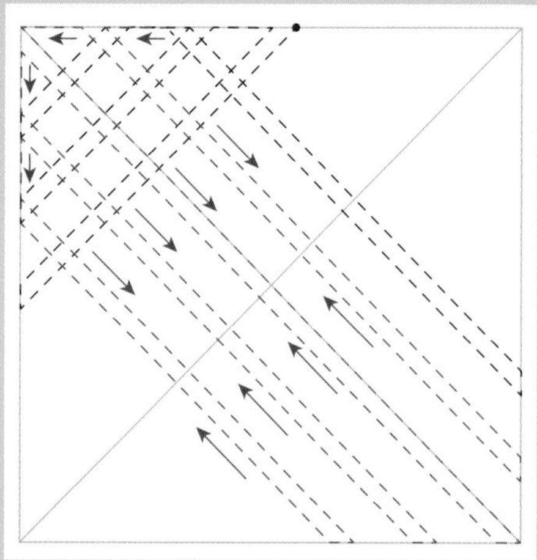

3

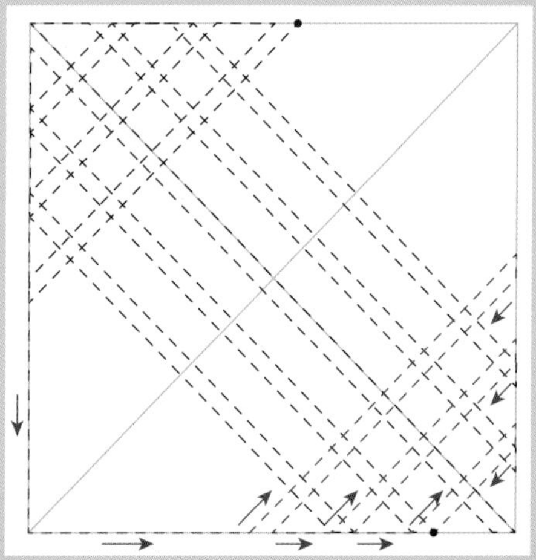

4

5

Heart Wreath

1

2

3

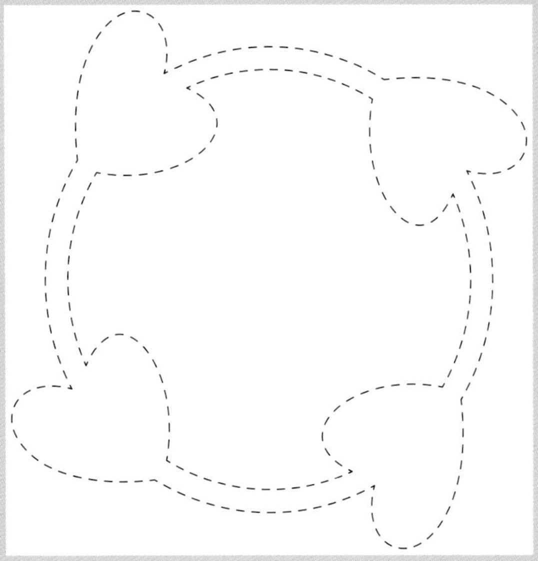

Posey Wreath 1

1
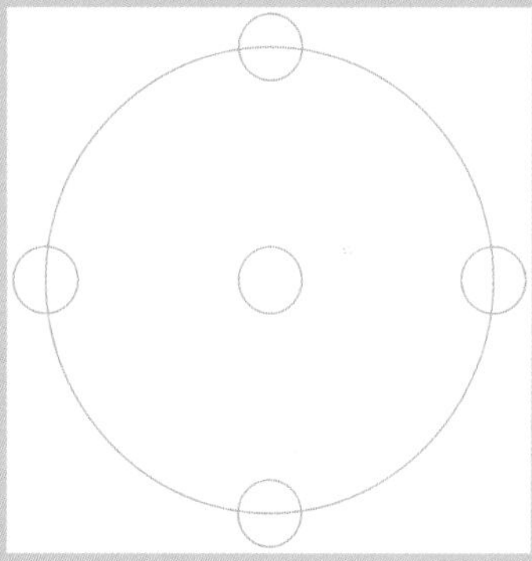

2
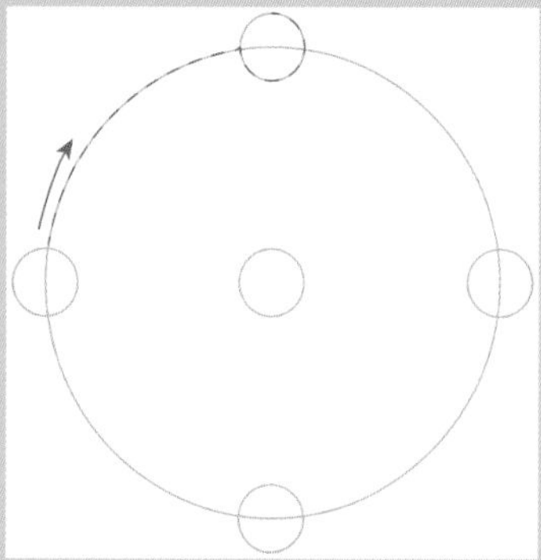

3
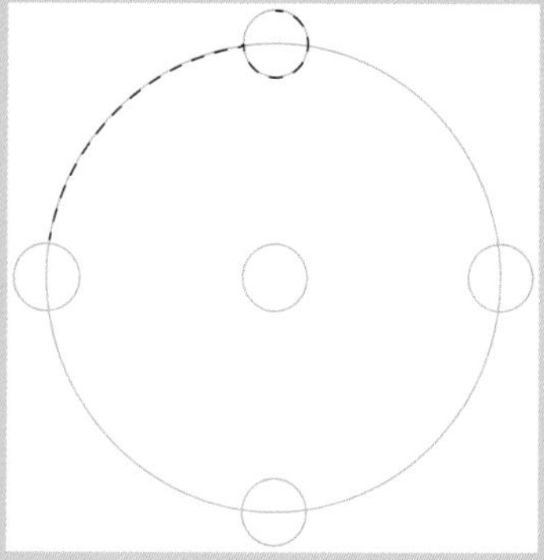

4
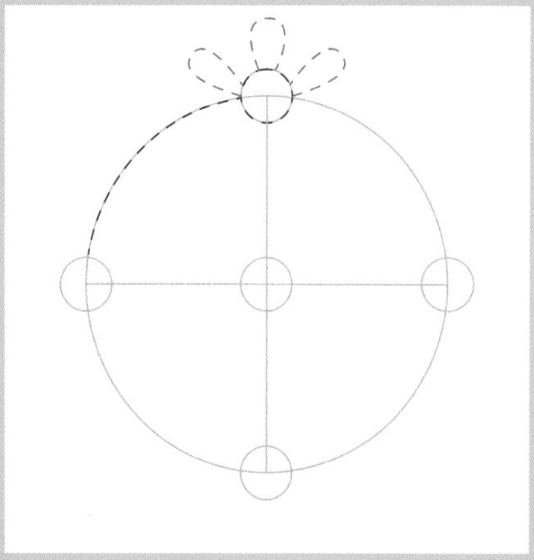

5
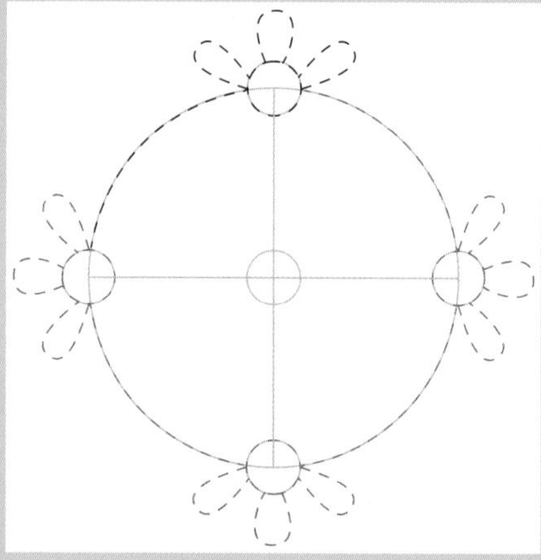

6

7

Posey Wreath 2

1

2
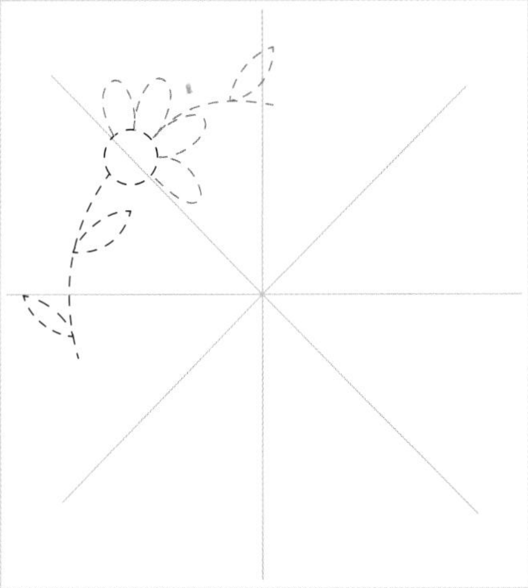

3
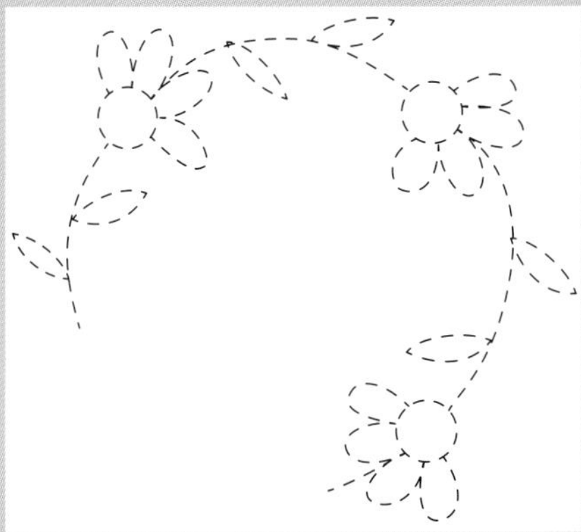

Leaf Wreath

Leaf Wreath with Buds

Leaf and Bud Variation

Chicken

1

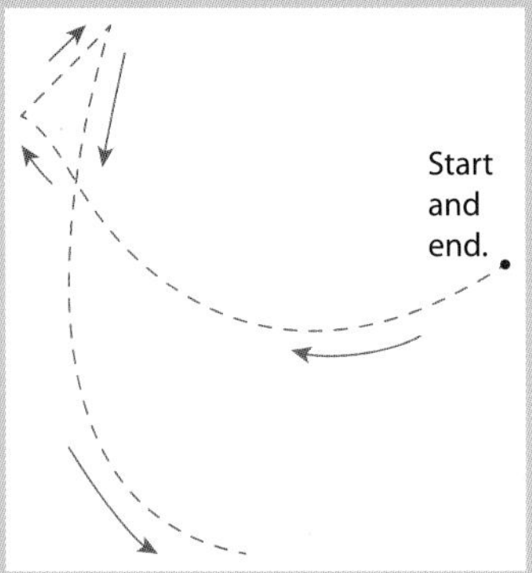

2

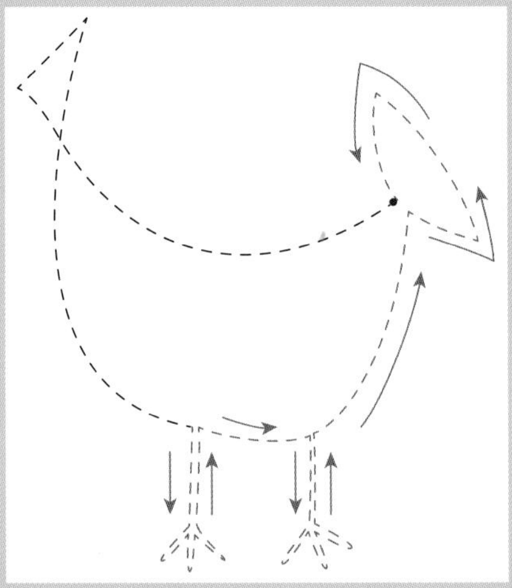

Diamond and Buds Wreath

1

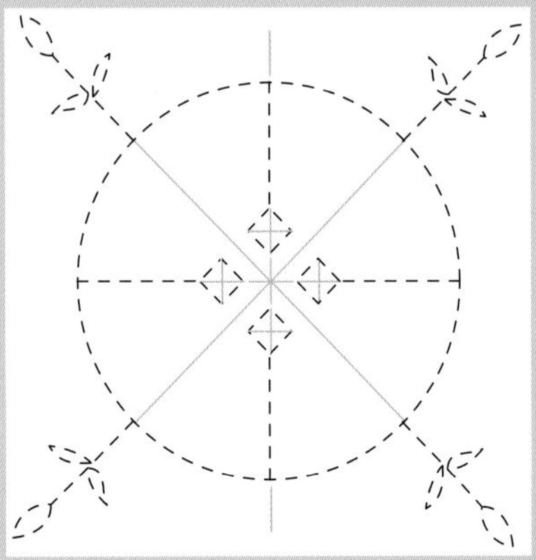

2

Tulip Wreath

Floral Star

1

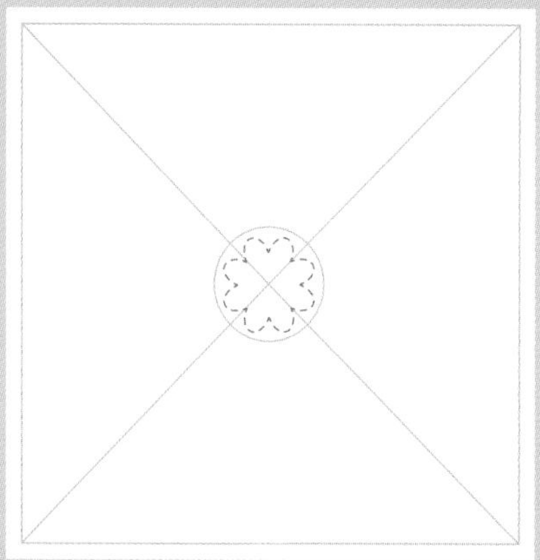

2

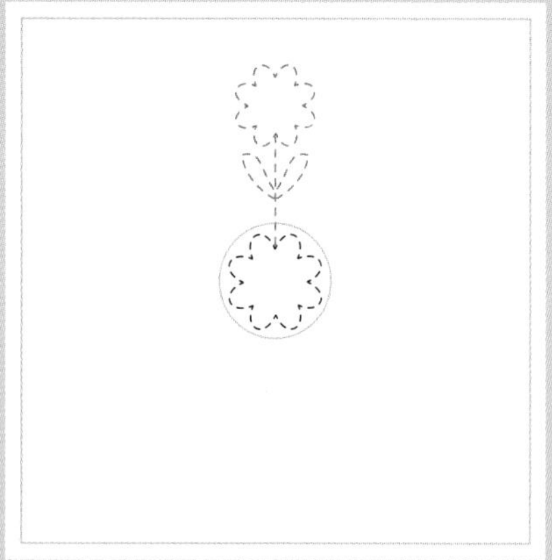

3

4

Diagonal Flowers

1

2

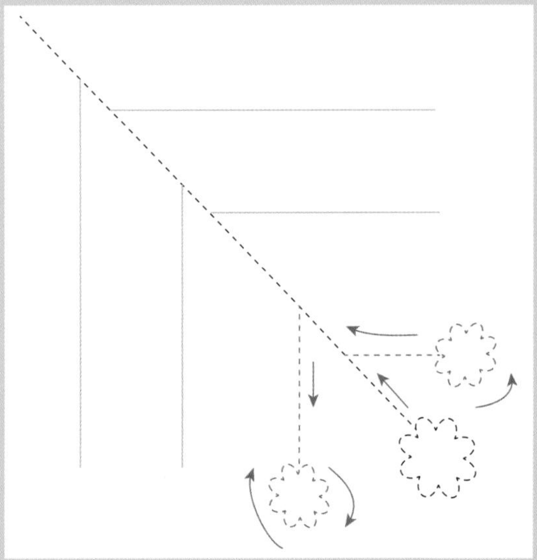

3

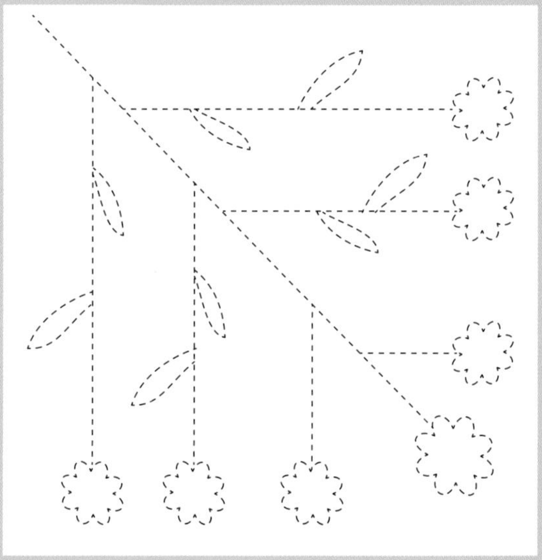

4

Flower Types and Formations

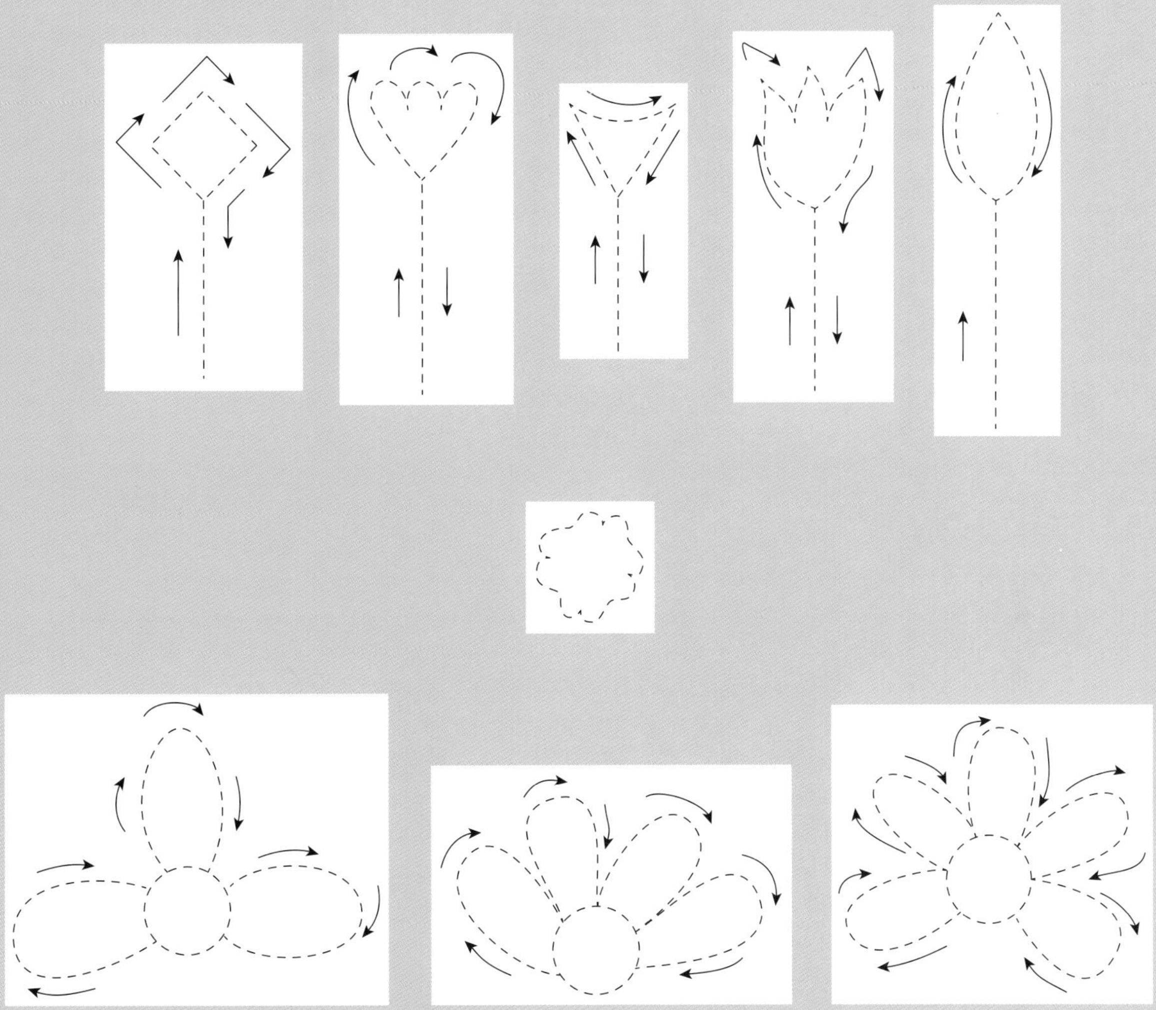

Floral Appliqué Quilt 1

Floral Appliqué Quilt 1, cottons, unknown maker, Eastern United States, c. 1860, 74″ × 94″

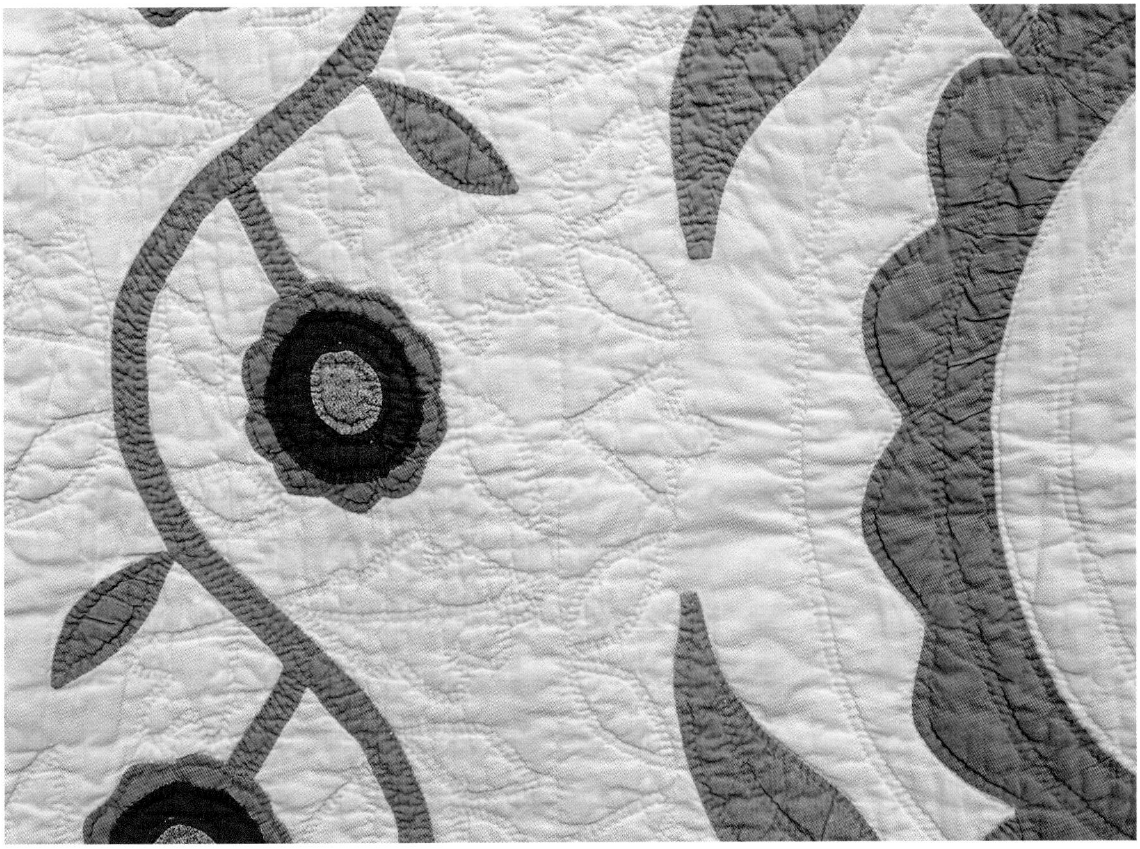

Floral appliqué quilts of the middle to late nineteenth century included bold, stylized motifs. The designs were decorative, graphic interpretations of natural elements. These graphic designs in fabric often included solid colors on a white background, enhanced with the texture of fine hand quilting.

Knowing the specifics about old quilts can lead to unbelievable finds, such as this 1860s floral appliqué quilt. It was bundled up on the floor in a shop in Portland, Oregon, in 2014, and the price was astonishingly low. Obviously, the seller had no idea what it really was.

It was in fact a magnificent example of a Civil War–era, six-block, floral appliqué quilt with a border, in almost pristine condition. A stunning bargain, its actual value was conservatively ten times the asking price. The quilt must have migrated to Oregon. It was so far out of its element, it took a knowledgeable buyer to recognize what it was. Now everyone can see what a wonderful quilt it is.

The relationship between the appliqué and quilting design is really wonderful. While the shapes of the quilting motifs are simple, an echoed outline really makes for an understated and elegant appearance.

Whirligig

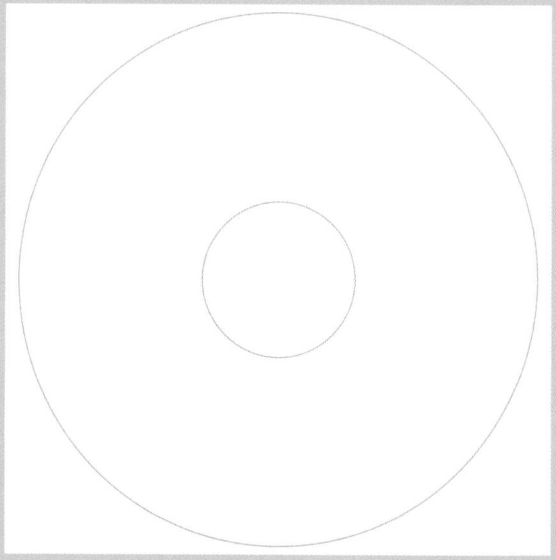

1

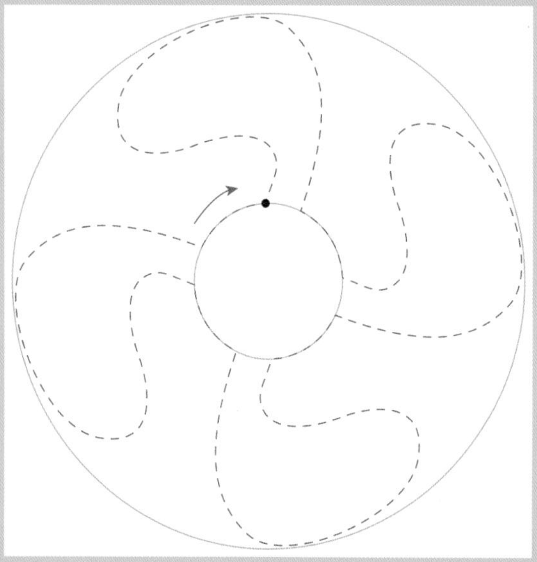

2

3

Oak Leaf

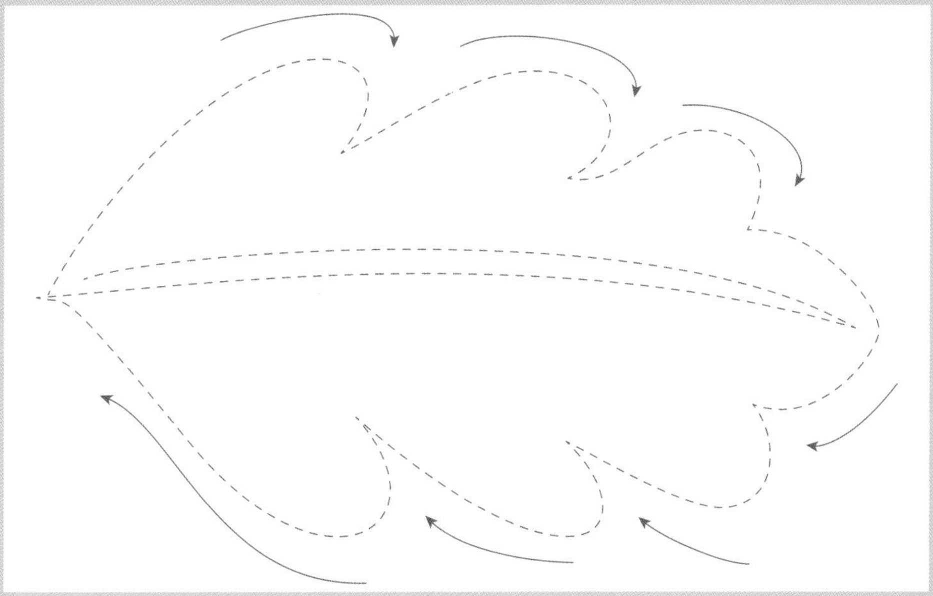
1

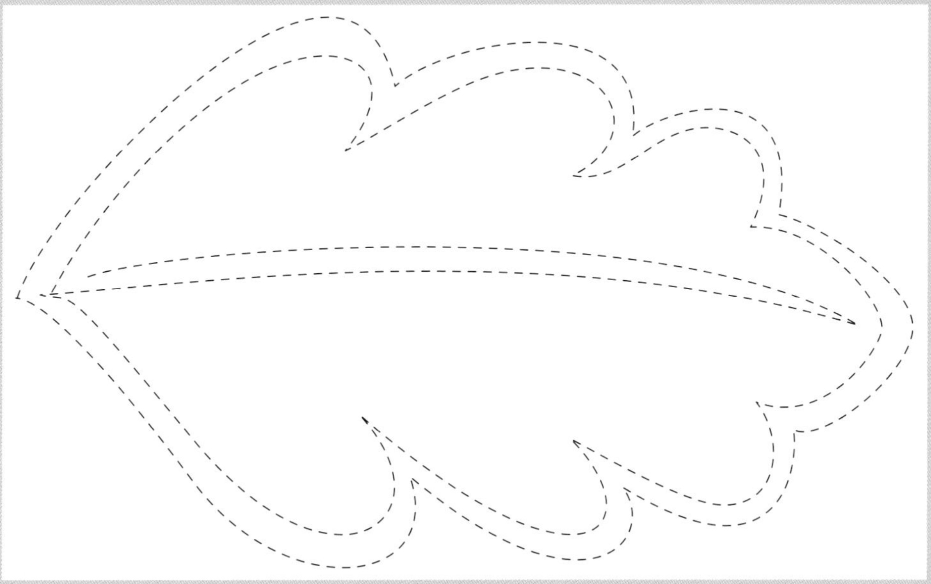
2

Leaf 1

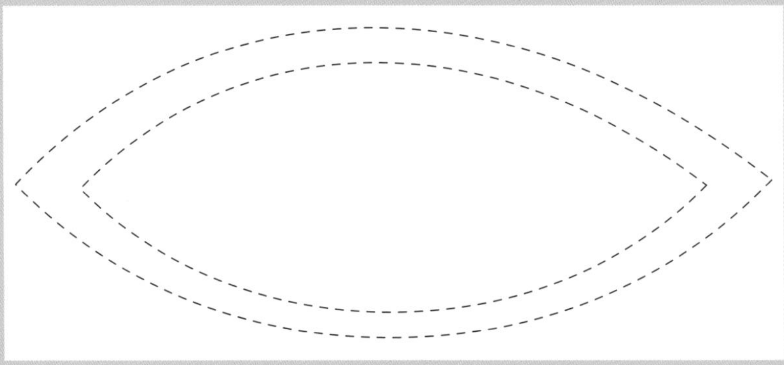

Leaf 2

Leaf 3

Quatrefoil

Floral Appliqué Quilt 2

Floral Appliqué Quilt 2; cottons; made by Mrs. M. E. Poyner; Paducah, Kentucky; c. 1860; 74″ × 86″

Quilt connoisseur Shelly Zegart discovered this quilt back in the early 1980s when she was one of the directors of the Kentucky Quilt Project, America's first statewide survey of quilts. It was in the collection of Hardin Pettit at the time. The quilt was eventually part of Zegart's collection and was touring with the Homefront & Battlefield: Quilts and Context in the Civil War exhibition when it was purchased by the Volckening Collection.

The motifs in floral appliqué quilts were often based on natural forms, but it was not always easy to recognize them later. For decades this quilt was called an Oak Leaf Variant for its similarities to other patchwork designs with oak leaves. On closer examination, it appeared to have elements of Christmas cactus and poke berries, possibly even amaryllis. The whimsical combination of motifs existed in the quilt, but not in nature.

DIAMOND CROSSHATCH

The diamond crosshatch in this quilt is a perfect example of simple quilting that recedes into the background, allowing the appliqué to shine. The easiest way to form a 30° diamond crosshatching is to use a prefabricated stencil and center it over the area you wish to fill, then marking the lines. If you are drawing this by hand, use a large gridded ruler for rotary cutting that has the angle you wish to use marked clearly. Line up along the edge of your block as you would for cutting fabric, and mark your first line. Mandy likes to mark the central lines first.

Prince's Feather Quilt

Prince's Feather Quilt, cottons, unknown maker, United States. c. 1850, 96″ × 96″

Prince's Feather is one of the earlier American appliqué designs. Like many other patterns of the period, it was inspired by botany. There is sometimes confusion about the name of the pattern, and people will call it Princess Feather, another name for the ornamental plant with the Latin name *Amaranthus hypochondriacus*.

This red and off-white Prince's Feather was discovered in a shop in Portland, Oregon. It was the same shop where the Floral Appliqué Quilt 1 (page 102) was found. Each of the nine spinning motifs have eight plumes surrounding a central, eight-pointed star. The border, with more plumes, stars, and fleur-de-lis motifs is unusual, as is the quilting with many leaves filling the negative space.

Echo Quilting

There are many ways to create an echo design, including varying the width between lines and bundling your lines. The corners of this quilt are set apart from the feather appliqué by circles made up of echoed lines, varying in distance from each other. The overall effect is quite stripey!

Two lines close together with a wider gap between them is often called *beadboard*.

Consistent spacing

Varied distance between lines

Single Motif Fill

This quilt is also an excellent example of how to take a single motif, in this case a leaf, and repeat it throughout to create a fill. First, decide on the shape or shapes you want, and use echoing to travel in between the locations where you want them to be. Experiment with the density and number of shapes.

note

This type of quilting does take some practice, so to avoid frustration, Mandy recommends taking it to the drawing board before you take it to the quilt top! Once you are comfortable drawing it out, then you're ready to quilt.

You may find it helpful to copy this page, and trace over the quilting path with your finger. Then try to fill in the rest of the sheet.

PUTTING IT ALL TOGETHER

It's pretty clear how these quilting designs can be used on a traditional quilt, but how do they apply to quilts that are more modern in their aesthetic? Mandy believes the leap is not a large one. Taking multiple elements from a variety of the quilts and creating a mash-up is an excellent way to create something fresh and new. Many modern quilts have large spaces to fill—why not treat them as if they were a wholecloth quilt, with the quilting designed to fill the space. Following are some examples Mandy created from the designs presented throughout the book.

Don't be afraid to make several patterns for yourself and play with layouts! Sometimes the best designs come from letting our mind go and seeing where your hands take you.

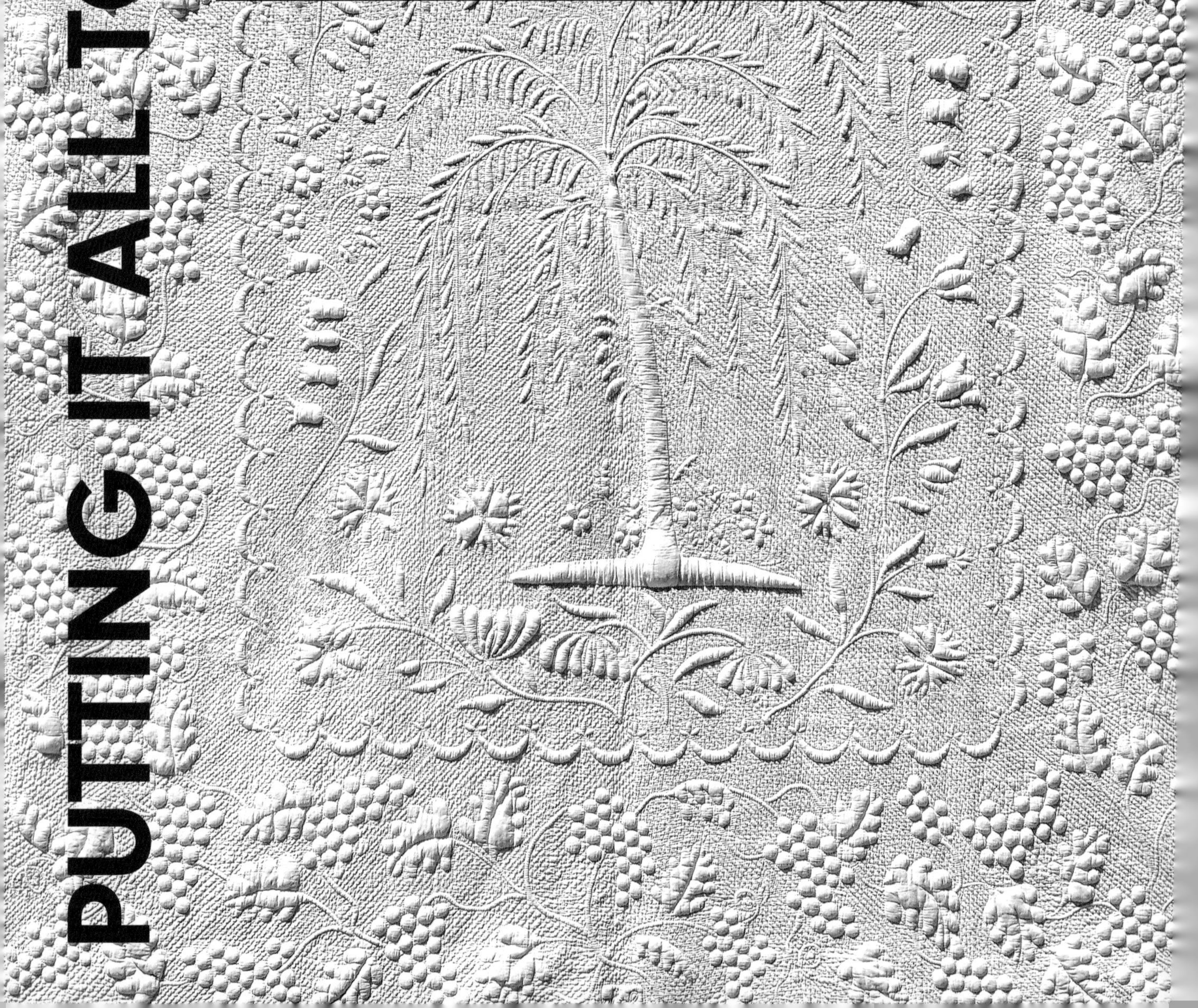

Combining Design Elements

FLORAL BORDER 1

The first border is inspired by the Album with Lyre Quilt (page 66). It is created in two steps, with the interior being quilted first. Feel free to choose any botanical design as you work your way along the outer spine.

The outer spine can be finished in a number of ways. Below, Mandy has finished it off to be the same as the top, echoing the spine and adding flowers and fruit as she did on the first. For a more "modern" treatment, consider replacing the fruit and flowers with bunches of circles.

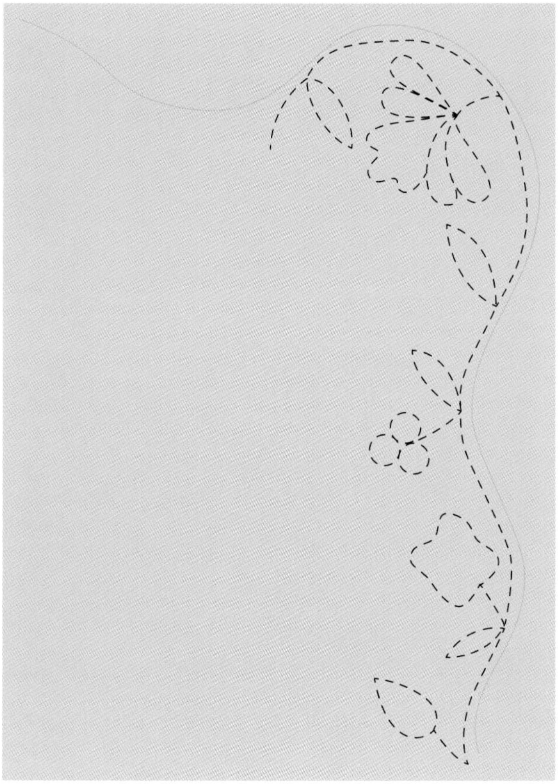

FLORAL BORDER 2

In this second option, Mandy chose to use the beadboard style of echoing to create an almost architectural finish. She envisions this type of border on the outermost edge of a quilt, with the inner border directing attention inward even as the exterior lines act as a natural frame.

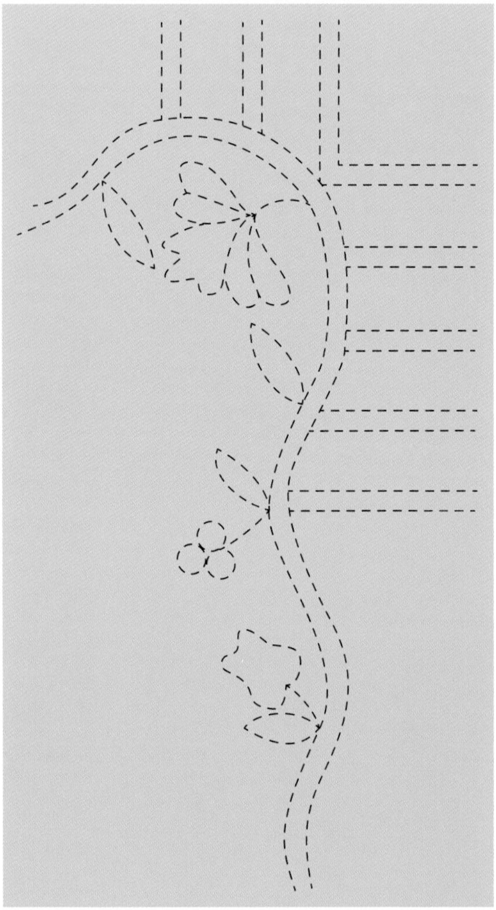

Beadboard

MODERN-LOOKING FLOWER

The flower below is actually a combination of a design from a border, the oval chain found in the Willow Tree Quilt 2 (page 55). Marking a central circle first, Mandy uses an overlapping oval just as she did in the chain to create large shallow petals. Echoed circles on the inside of varying widths makes for a most interesting and modern-looking flower.

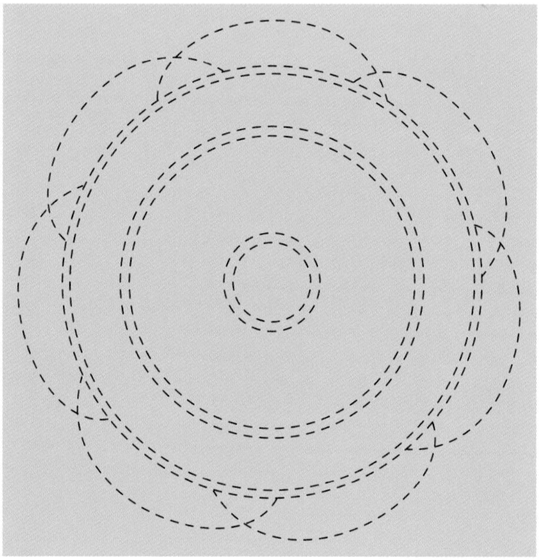

POMEGRANATE BORDER

In the next example, Mandy uses the pomegranate design from the Album with Lyre Quilt (page 66) to create a repetitive border of pomegranates, which also has a very elegant look. Changing up the interior of the corner circle can also make the border have a little bit of oomph.

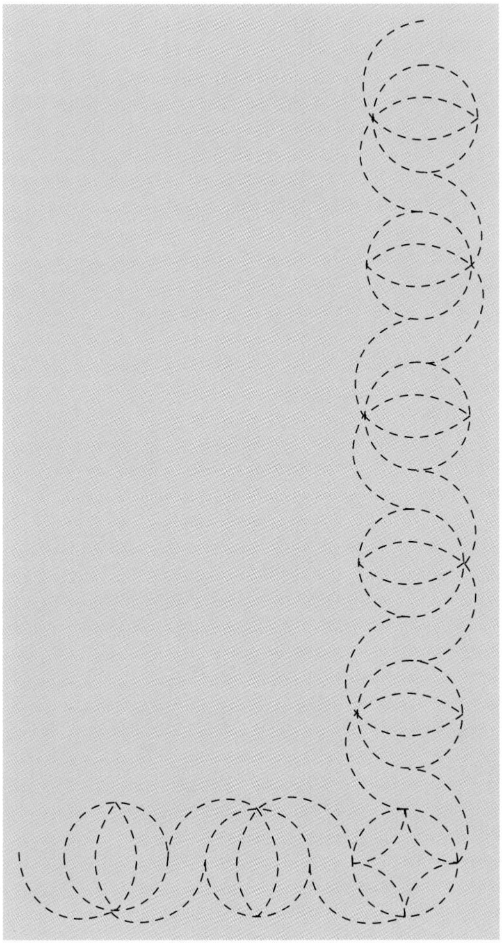

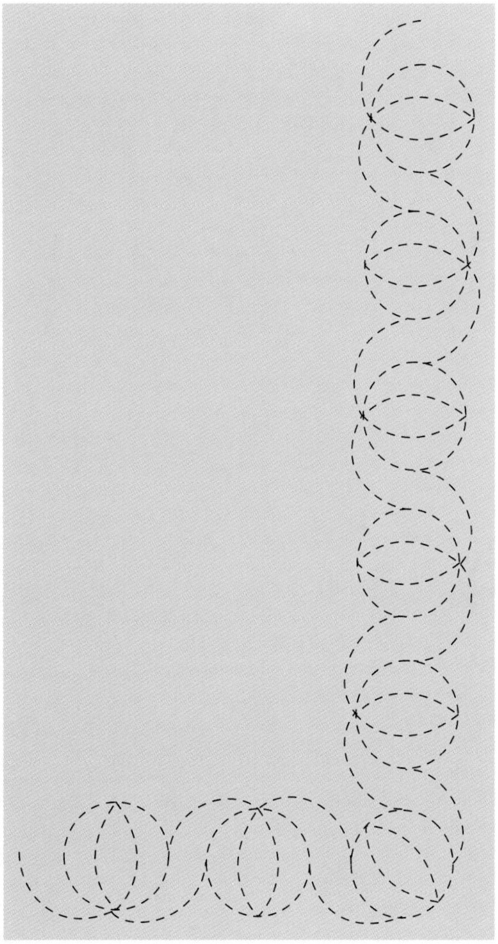

ABSTRACT GRAPES IN FOUR VARIATIONS

When looking at an old quilt for inspiration, sometimes it's helpful to squint your eyes and look for shapes. That's how Mandy came up with these designs based on the grapes from the Willow Tree Quilt 1 (page 54) from the Willow Tree Quilt 2 (page 55). Realizing that the grapes were often in triangular bunches, Mandy wanted to play on that idea. While the following border motifs are inspired by the Willow Tree quilts, it was only after she drew them out that Mandy realized she had seen this type of design before—on jewelry from Ancient Greece!

A word of caution, though, pebbles and pearls are time-consuming to quilt, so plan accordingly!

First, a simple geometric abstraction and a quilting path.

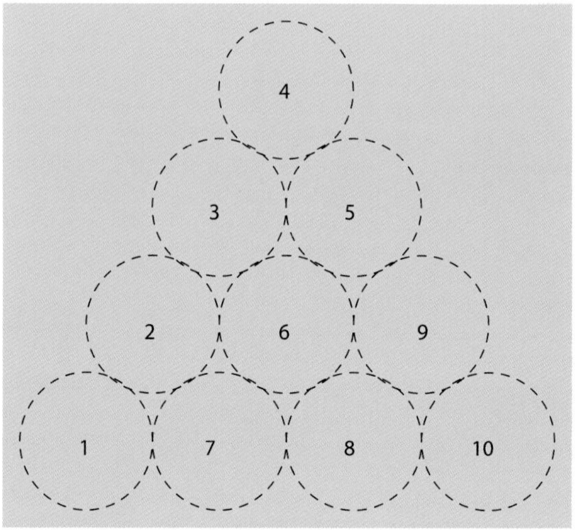

And because the grapes were essentially an equilateral triangle, there's an opportunity to create interesting designs, such as a six-pointed star using a hexagon base.

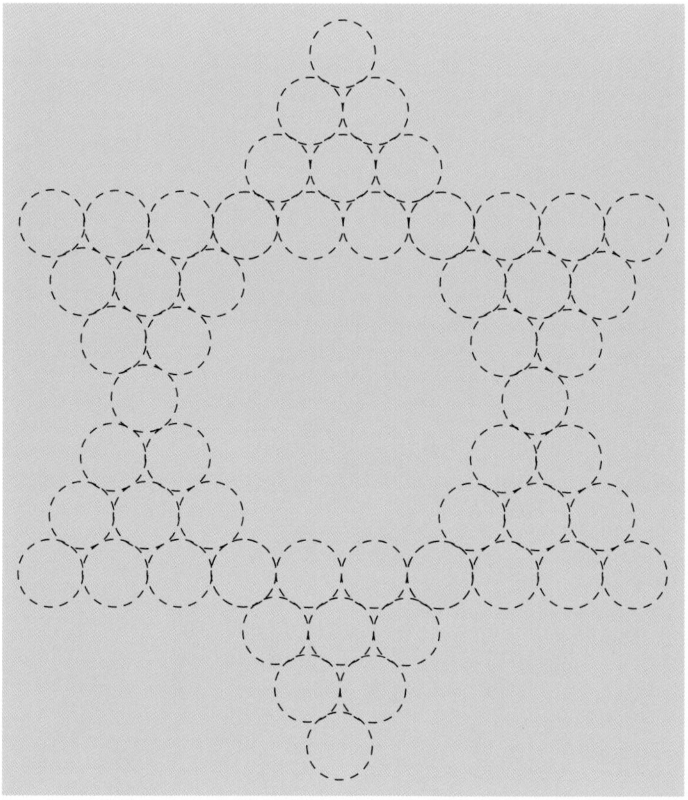

By repeating the base shape, you can also turn it into an interesting background fill.

Or even as border treatments.

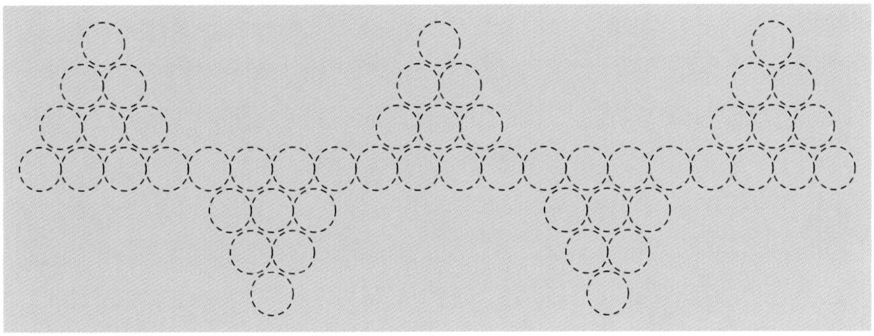

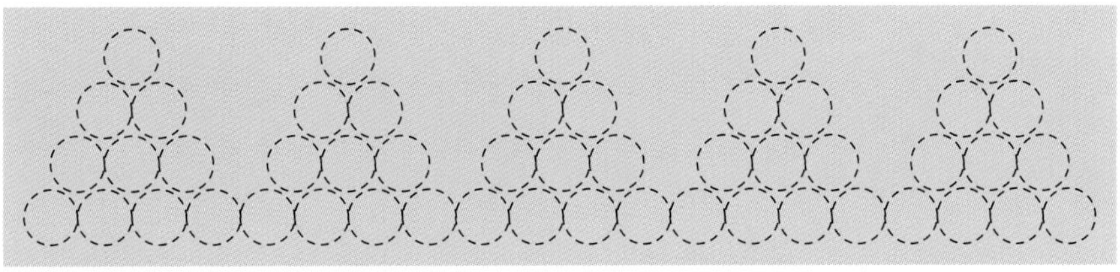

FLOWER IN A BROKEN GRID

This is one of Mandy's favorite ideas from working with Bill's quilts. With such large spaces to fill in many modern quilts, the echoed crosshatch grid from the Appliqué Sampler with Wreaths and Birds Quilt (page 88) paired with a single floral motif such as the Peony from the Willow Tree Quilt 2 (page 55) are a great pairing of designs. Breaking the line of the grid so that the flower seems to float freely also creates a visual break from more traditional quilting designs.

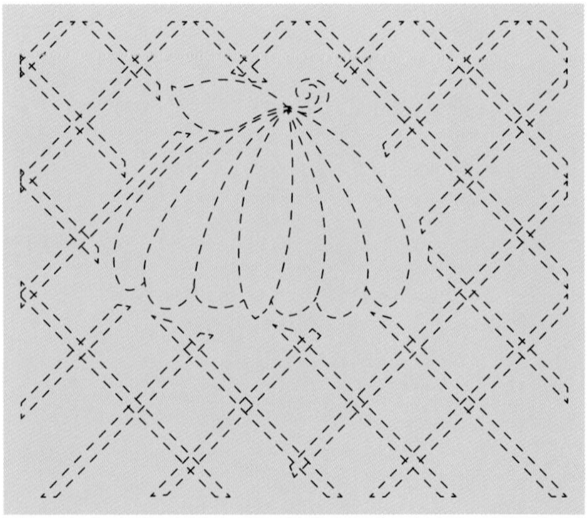

THISTLES FOR MILES

Straight-line quilting is ubiquitous. To make it more her own, Mandy takes elements from the quilt top or fabric and incorporates them into the lines in silhouette. At right, Mandy has taken the thistle from the Album with Lyre Quilt (page 66) and split it into two halves, one half on each straight line. The design is striking and can be made subtler with a greater spacing between the flower elements.

Being able to break apart the elements of a design and then create a mash-up takes practice and a sense of playfulness. If you see something you like in a quilting design, stop and ask yourself what about it really grabs your attention? Can you break it up into pieces, and then put them together in a different way?

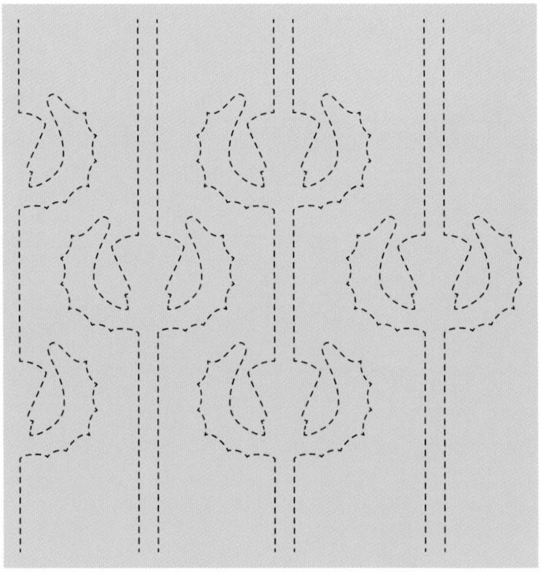

Design Patterns

The following patterns are the backbone for forming many of the designs in the book. They are not meant to be permanent, but instead act as a reference point to help make your design balanced and accurate. You can easily draw them yourself; make copies of these pages, sizing them as needed; or purchase stencils that are available for marking in the guides you want.

CIRCLE DIVISION

With the first lines placed on the horizontal and vertical axe, at 90°, the diagonal lines are exactly 45°. You can choose different sizes of circle to place over the top to help determine where quilting lines will cross over. This example has a circle in the middle.

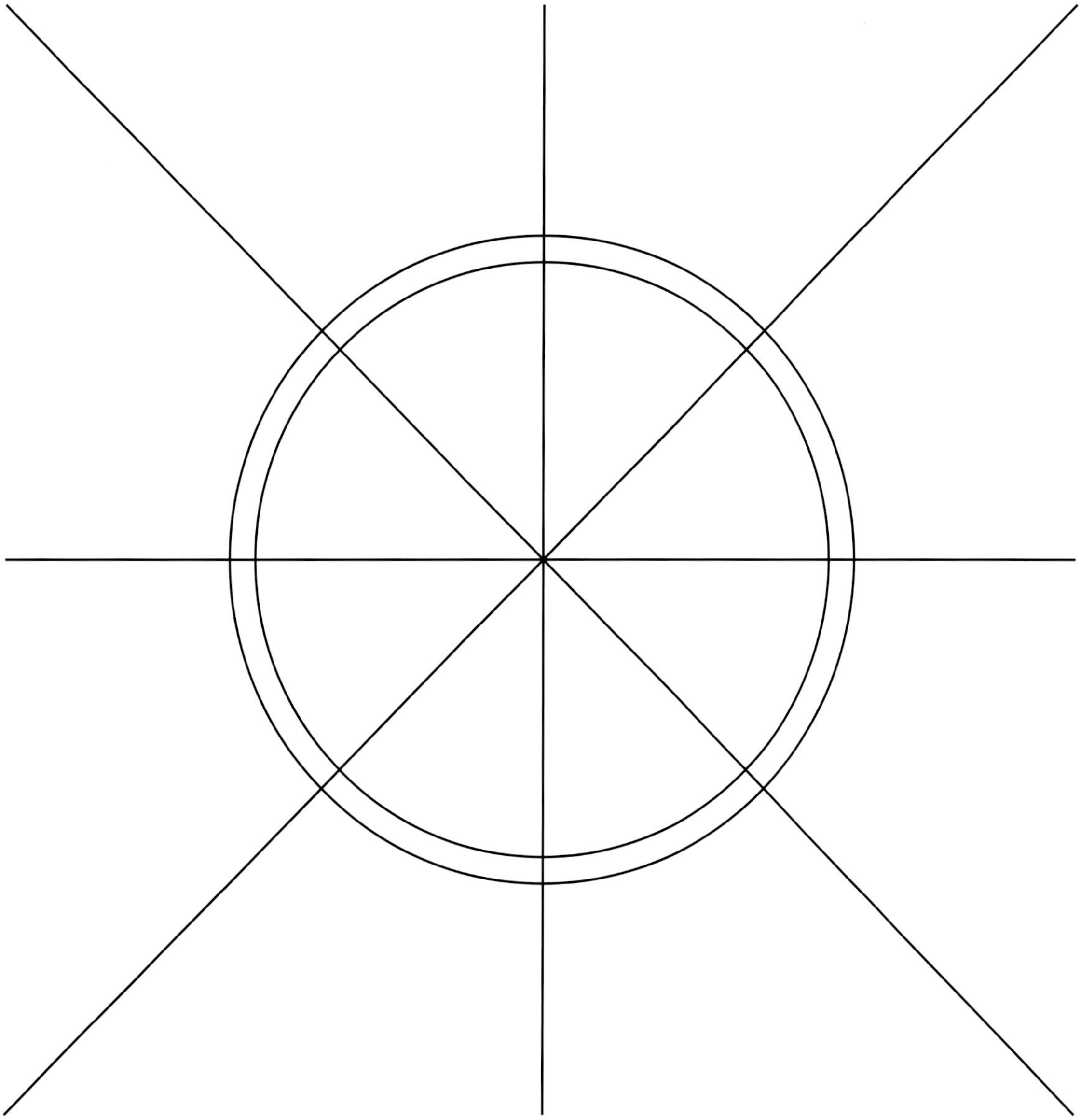

SQUARE DIVISION

Use for visualizing square-in-square designs or dividing blocks into eighths.

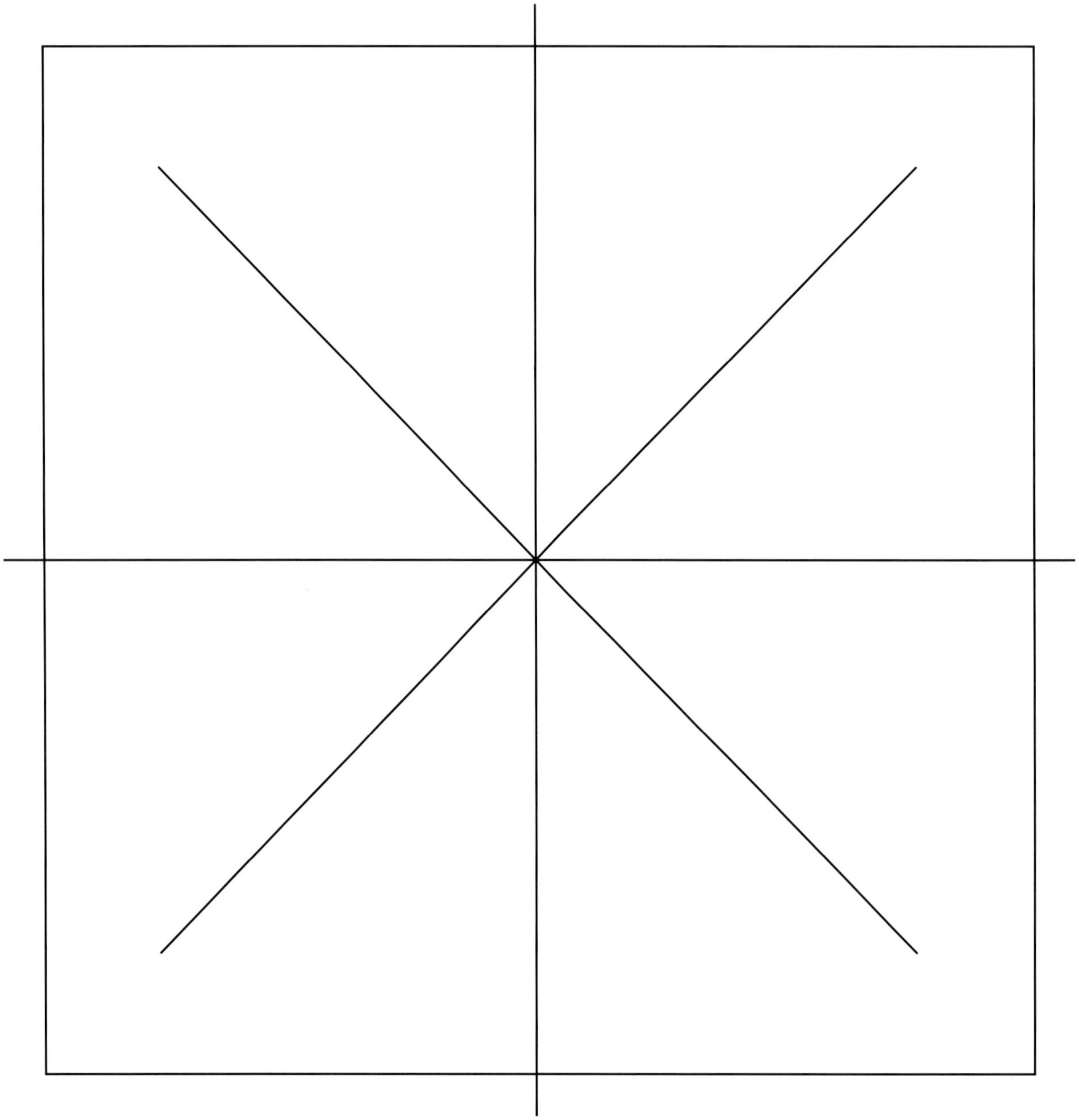

Also divided into eight wedges of 45°, but not on the vertical and horizontal axes, the look of the finished design based upon this will have different visual qualities.

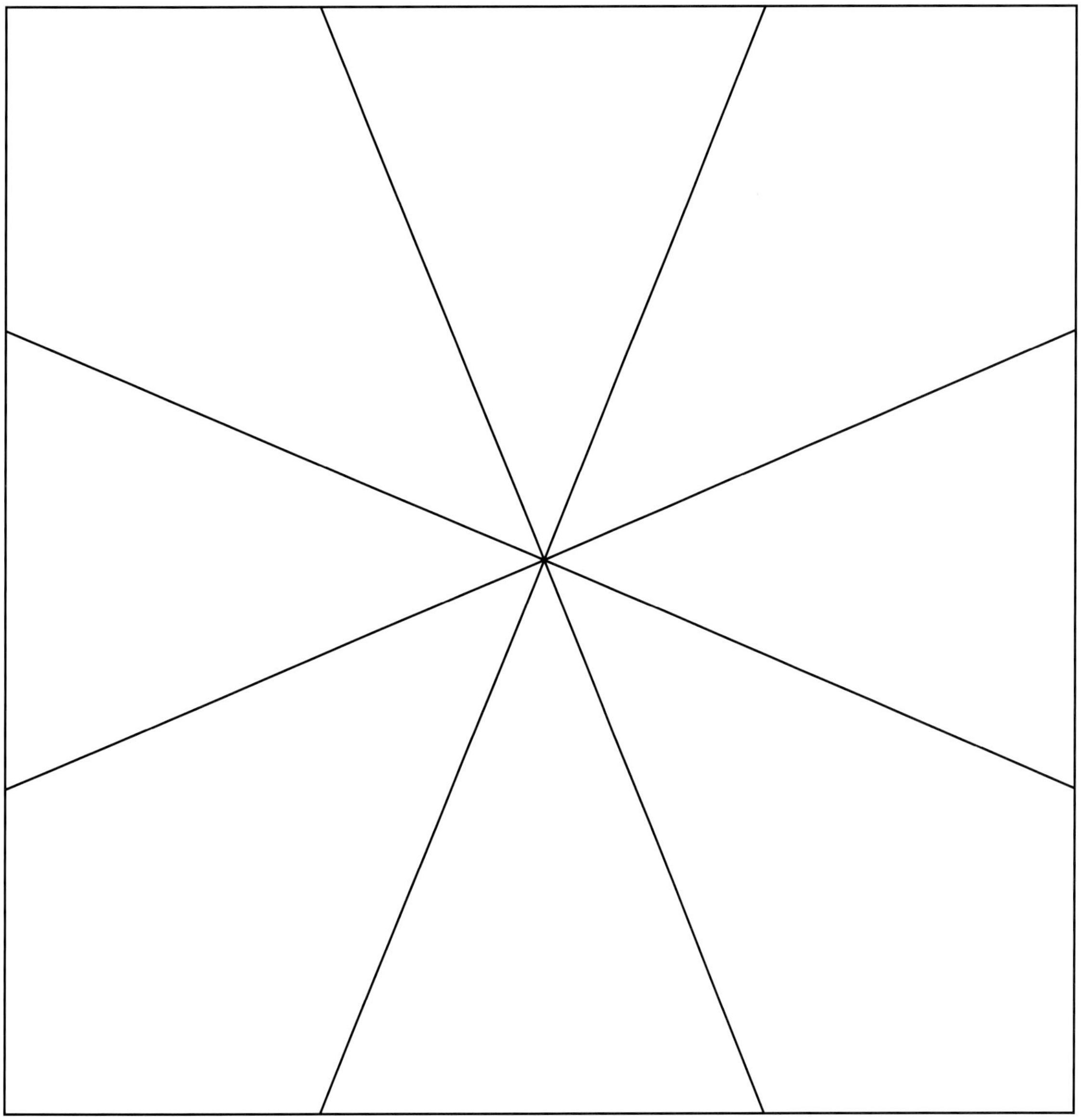

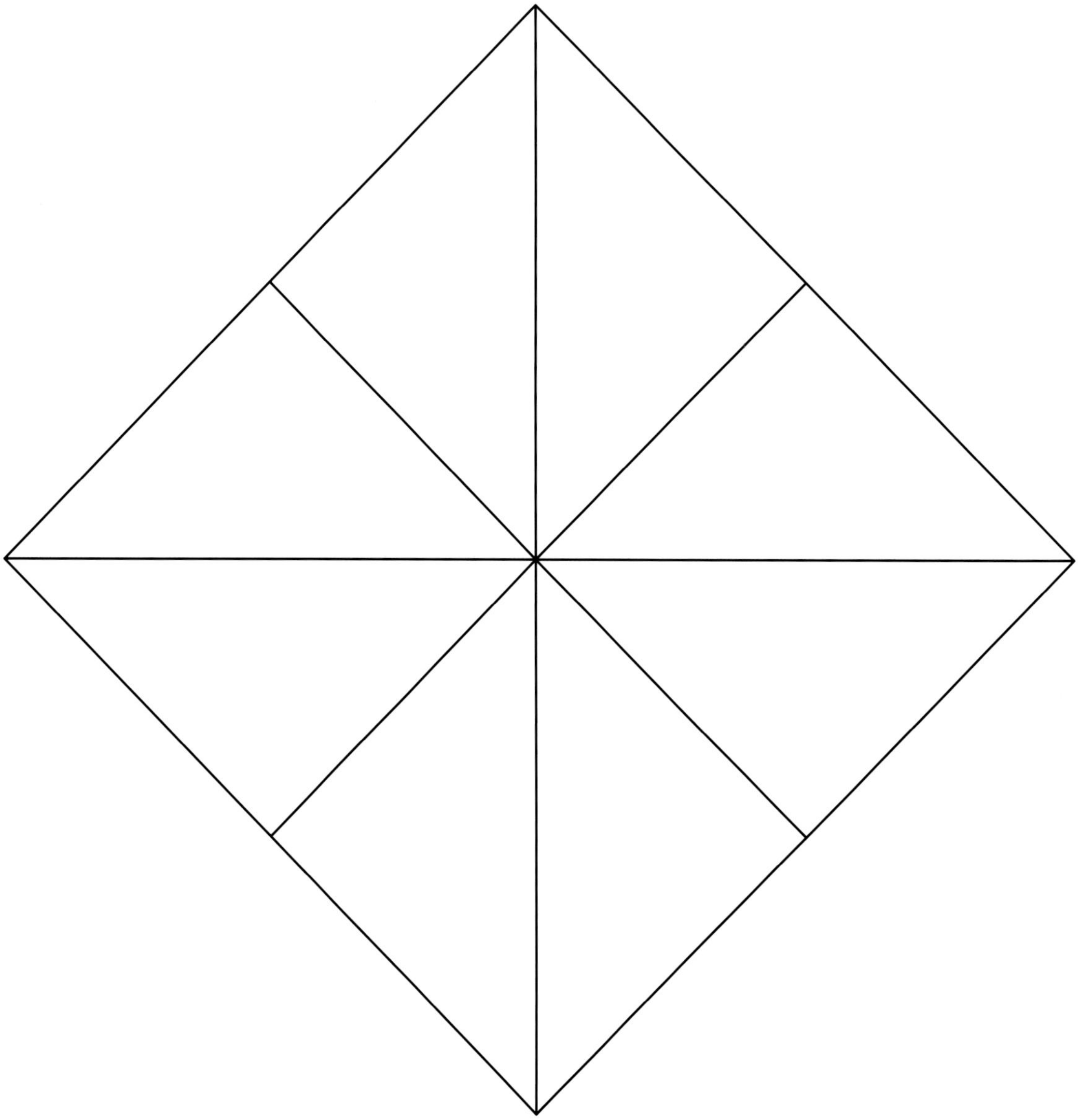

VINE AND FEATHERS

The following pattern is for forming the spines of vines and feathers. To draw your own, divide up your space as you wish (the pattern below shows the divisions in even increments vertically). Next, determine the height of your spine. Mandy likes to draw guidelines at a 45° angle for the feathers every so often, especially if her goal is to quilt feathers as uniformly as possible.

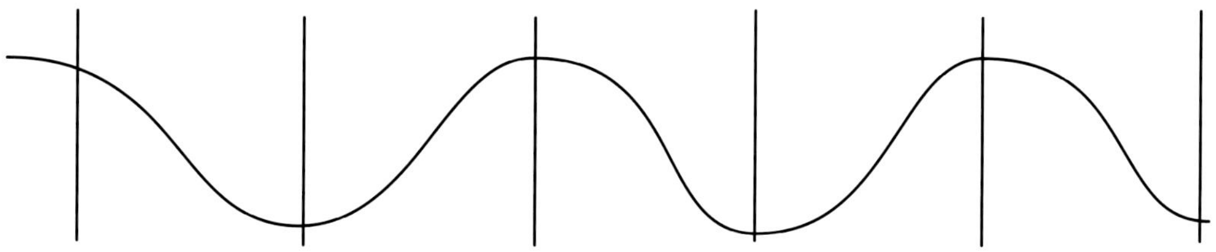

HEART-SHAPED MEDALLIONS

To use one of these designs, trace it onto stiff paper or template plastic, then cut it out along the lines.

Simple Heart Medallion

This pattern is for the Simple Heart Medallion (page 26). Notice it is a square on point. The template you will create is one-quarter of the entire design and must be repeated 4 times.

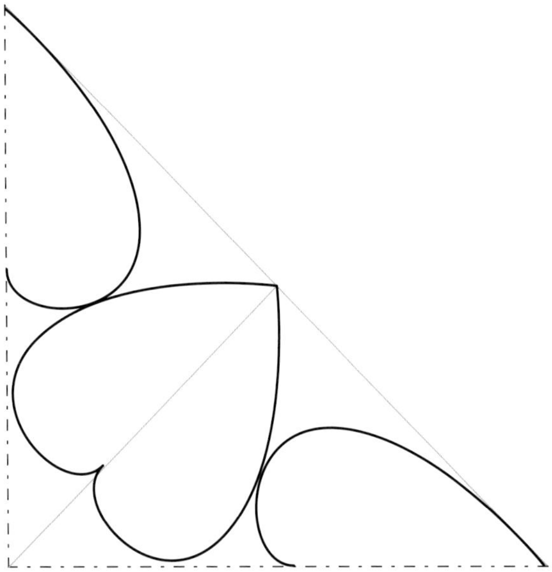

Stacked Heart Medallion

This pattern is for the Stacked Heart Medallion (page 70). The template you will create is one-eighth of the entire design. For detailed instructions on how to use this pattern, see page 70.

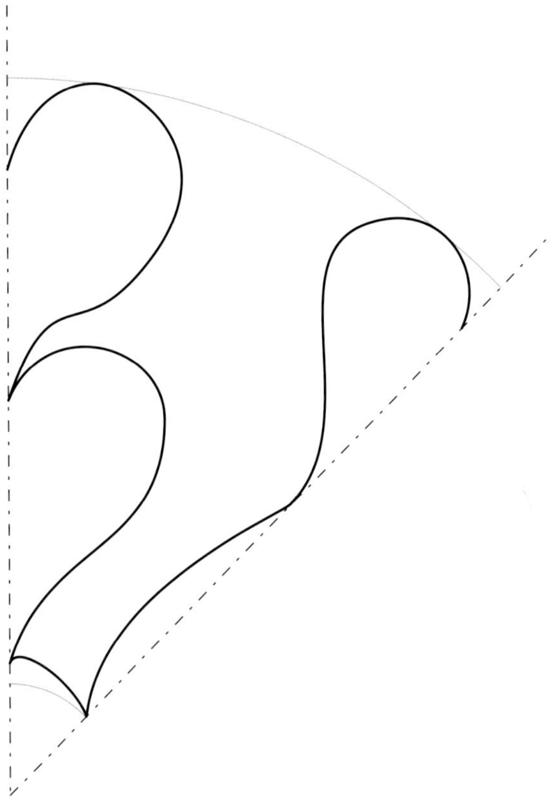

About the Authors

Photo by Bill Volckening

Bill Volckening calls himself a quilt magnet—he has an uncanny ability to find great quilts. Bill studied at Rhode Island School of Design (1984–1986), School of Visual Arts (BFA 1988), and was part of a select graduate program at New York University and the International Center of Photography (MA 1991).

Bill's award-winning blog, *Wonkyworld*, reveals the process of collecting from the perspective of a twenty-first-century collector. It is about the thrill of the hunt, the bounty, and the unfolding story of his remarkable quilt journey. Bill is also an award-winning photographer and quiltmaker, and his work has been published globally. Quilts from his collection have been exhibited from New York to Tokyo and have appeared in various publications worldwide.

Bill has authored two previous books: *New York Beauty, Quilts from the Volckening Collection in 2015* (by Quiltmania) and *Modern Roots—Today's Quilts from Yesterday's Inspiration* (by Stash Books).

Photo by Jessica Bizzarro Photography

Once upon a time, **Amanda Leins** was studying for a PhD in classical archaeology. She went as far from home as she could. She studied ancient languages and classical literature. She studied material culture (the remains of human activity in the archaeological record), art history, and modern ethical questions about how to deal with what was dug up. She excavated in Israel and studied ceramics in Rome, and then headed back to the United States, where she met and married her best beloved, making a new life.

She had left her PhD program and it was during a visit with her grandparents in 2002 that Amanda discovered quilting—her Grampa Johnny's love of quilts and textiles influenced her decision to head down to the local quit shop with Gramma that day.

Her quilting journey is about all these things: family and traditions, modern and traditional techniques, ancient and contemporary histories, and how we include all these in our craft. She purchased her first longarm in 2012 and now teaches and speaks on all things quilting at quilt shows and guilds across the United States. Her studio is located in Saratoga Springs, New York.

MORE FROM BILL VOLCKENING:

Website: billvolckening.com

Blog: willywonkyquilts.blogspot.com

MORE FROM AMANDA LEINS:

Website: mandalei.com

Available as an eBook only

Want even more creative content?
Go to ctpub.com/offer
& sign up to receive our gift to you!
MENU
C&T PUBLISHING
Your Home for Creative Quilting & Sewing
HAND PRINTING STUDIO
Print on Almost Anything!
Get some in-spiration
GET INSPIRED
GARMENT SEWING LOOKBOOK 2016
Make it, snap it, share it
using
#ctpublishing